What oth... ... . this book:

"Ms. Mikatavage recognizes the admirable qualities which characterize the immigrant spirit. This book provides signposts along the road to successful adjustment and promotes self-confidence."
— **Patricia A. Hatch, founder of FIRN, Foreign-born Information and Referral Network, Inc.**

"Easy to understand, straightforward, and often humorous."
— **Leslie D. Norris, Migration and Refugee Services, U.S. Catholic Conference**

"References and information stimulate creative thinking and provide teachers with ways to incorporate life skills in their teaching... valuable guidelines for success that could be utilized by any learner — not just the foreign-born."
— **Jennifer Singer-Reed, Coordinator of Adult Literacy Services, Carroll County Public Schools, Maryland**

"Valuable insights and explanations of cultural differences, expressed without hostility or condescension."
— **Amy Southwick, Reference & Database Librarian and ESL teacher**

"This book will help you find a new world, without losing yourself in it."
— **Dr. Jonas Jasaitis, Editor, *DIRVA - The Lithuanian National Newspaper***

"The text addresses a number of topics of importance to immigrants and refugees attempting to adjust to life in the United States. Designed for an adult audience, the text offers insights into and explanations for many of the cultural differences... examines practical and financial topics of concern."
— **James Estes, Research Associate, National Clearinghouse for Bilingual Education**

"Much-needed information for immigrants who want to settle in quickly...full of resources and proven strategies for a quick adjustment."
— **Judy Priven, author of *Hello! USA* and *Hello! Washington***

IMMIGRANTS & REFUGEES

Create Your New Life in America

Raimonda Mikatavage

Pioneer Living Series®

Melodija Books

Also by Raimonda Mikatavage
Your Journey to Success: A Guide for Young Lithuanians
Tavo Kelias i Sekme (in Lithuanian)

International customers: the toll-free (800 or 888) telephone numbers in this book can only be dialed from within the continental United States.

For international rights and foreign translations, please contact the publisher.
Melodija Books, P.O. Box 689, Hampstead, MD 21074 USA
Tel: (410) 374-3117 Fax: (410) 374-3569.
Internet: http://www.melodija.com   E-mail: books@melodija.com

Cover design: Paul Erickson *www.ericksonline.com*
Book design and production: Mayapriya Long   *www.mindspring.com/~bookwrights*

Publisher's Cataloging-in-Publication
(Provided by Quality Books, Inc.)

Mikatavage, Raimonda.
    Immigrants and Refugees: create your new life in America /
by Raimonda Mikatavage. —2nd. ed., rev.
    p. cm. — (Pioneer living series)
    Includes bibliographical references and index.
    Library of Congress Catalog Card Number: 98-65061
    ISBN 0-9647213-5-X

    1. Success. 2. Immigrants—United States—Life skills guides.
    3. Refugees—United States—Life skills guides. 4. Americanization.
    I. Title. II. Title: Immigrants and refugees

BJ1611.M55 1998   158'.089
                                              QBI98-90

CONTENTS

ACKNOWLEDGMENTS

Many people were involved in making this book possible. They have contributed their expertise, constructive critique, and much-needed encouragement. They are listed below in alphabetical order.

Richard Arbogast
Jeannette Belliveau
Tatyana Bernadskay
Frank J. Bien
Amphay Borravong
Silvina Cassinelli
Elizabeth Claire
Mark Dialectos
Mary Zervanos-Dialectos, Esq.
Aleksandr Elbert
Officer Doug Gibson
Patricia A. Hatch
Dr. Jonas Jasaitis
Regina Kaufmann
Barbara Karl
Marina Kravchenko
Adolfo Lopez, MD
Arthur Lukowski
Linda Matthews
Bernice Mikatavage

Beltran Navarro
Sister Mary Neil
Carmen Nieves
Dienlan Nguyen
Leslie D. Norris
Eugenia Ordynsky, Esq.
Rudy Paul
Judy Priven
Vivian B. Rymer
Kinza Schuyler
Alison Seiler
Leo Shraybman
Jennifer Singer-Reed
Lidia Soto-Harmon
Amy Southwick
Bernard Terway
Kara Uleman
Meintje Westerbeek
Roger P. Winter
World Relief staff

Thank you to *Darbininkas*, the Lithuanian weekly newspaper, for the permission to reprint the humorous anecdotes.

And always, special thanks to James T. Mikatavage, my husband and best friend.

INTRODUCTION

Why You Need This Book

This book is for all pioneers. Webster's dictionary provides this definition of the word <u>pioneer:</u> "One who opens up new areas of thought, research, or development." Modifying this definition to pertain to you and me — immigrants to this country — we can say that, <u>as pioneers, we must launch new thoughts and actions to build our own quality life.</u>

Not every immigrant who comes to America fits the definition of a pioneer. Many don't. A typical immigrant story often goes like this: A family of four arrives to the U.S., selected under the visa diversity plan (green card lottery). Their intentions for coming are to obtain better education for the children, better job opportunities, better standard of living. All noble intentions.

As any family, the newcomers will make many decisions. Will these decisions be made with a lot of personal reflection, with calculated risk, carried through with thoughtful action? Well, no. It is often easier to just continue doing what they used to do in their country or what they see the people around them doing.

Years go by. The immigrant family adapts here and there. The parents come to a realization that life in America is complicated and difficult, not easier than in their own country, in fact, in many ways harder. They are proud of some things, but regret others. They often feel lonely. They are not satisfied with their lives, but will rarely admit it. They didn't expect things to be like this, but going back to their country is unthinkable after all this time. They will be viewed as failures by their relatives and besides, they are too "Americanized" by now. The focus turns to the children. At least they speak English well. Let them get a good education and satisfying jobs. We came here for them anyway, didn't we?

What has happened? Well, the typical immigrant story, with all its initial promise and hope, with the passing years, turns into an often typical American story. Important life choices are made with little thought, by accident, or with the wrong intentions. Bad habits get a strong hold on daily existence. Poor social skills prevent meaningful relationships. Lack of knowledge about money prevents a secure future. The immigrant story turns sour. True satisfaction in the land of opportunity becomes unreachable. It happens all the time.

As you already know, starting a new life in a new country is hugely demanding. A newcomer may become so overwhelmed with all the pressures – new language, finding work, learning how to get around, getting acclimated, and often feeling either excited or depressed – that the intention becomes to just make it through another day.

Yes, you made a decision to move to America. And yes, you did what it takes to get here. Congratulations! Most likely, many from your country tried to come here but failed. However, we can all make mistakes in life. Our decision to come to this country is <u>not immune</u> from being a potential mistake. Whether it becomes or remains "a mistake" will depend on what we do <u>now</u>, now that we are here.

You may call yourself a newcomer, an immigrant, a refugee, an American, or you may still identify yourself most strongly with the country of your origin. However you choose to identify yourself, whether you can call yourself a <u>pioneer</u>, depends on your willingness to <u>launch new thoughts and actions</u>. Believing, thinking and acting as you did in your country, may or may not have usefulness here. Your willingness to accept, adapt and change will greatly determine your ability to find the "better life" you came to find. Becoming an American will not give you lasting satisfaction. Becoming a pioneer will.

This book is not all inclusive or meant to be the final authority on life in America. It doesn't warn you of all the obstacles, surprises or pitfalls that lie ahead. (Just think of all the surprises your homeland would pose to any newcomer!) However, this book offers some proven strategies that could help prepare you for some major decisions, that could prevent some mistakes, that could save you money, that could solve some problems.

After reading this book, you must seek out as much additional knowledge as possible <u>on all subject areas, not just the ones that interest you</u>. There are many sad stories about immigrants who, by not broadening their general knowledge about their new life, got in deep trouble with taxes, failed in their career goals, went bankrupt, and experienced other tragedies. <u>You need to know more than just what is in front of you.</u>

<u>Dear Pioneer, your decision to move here will most certainly have permanent consequences. I hope your actions lead you to a most satisfying, pioneering life in America.</u>

Closure

"Without dreams of hope and pride a man will die. Though his flesh still moves, his heart sleeps in the grave..." — song clip, Chuck Mangione.

Psychologists believe that the basic necessities of a human being include security, recognition, control over one's life, and a need for creative expression and new experiences. (M. Scott Peck, 1978.) In my country of origin, Lithuania, the people had been violated by the soviet occupation in every basic human necessity, and not just for a day, or a week, but for 50 years. There was no freedom to experience, to speak the truth, to create what you want, to live on your own terms.

Perhaps your country was violated in one way or another. Perhaps that's why you are here. Perhaps you have come to America angry about having to start all over. If that is the case, you will want to have closure on those feelings. It won't help you to keep blaming someone else and to keep waiting for things to get better in your country so you can go back. You are here now. If your thoughts are always <u>there</u>, how can you achieve success <u>here</u>? In the words of Barry Tuckwell, a successful, Australian-born musician and a new U.S. citizen, "It's like getting married. If you're going to be in a country, don't do it with your suitcase packed." (Baltimore Sun, 1996.)

Try not to live your life one foot in America, one foot in your homeland. Of course, you will never forget your country or the relatives that still remain there. You can stay in touch by letters, phone calls, occasional visits, but when you are here, be <u>here.</u> Your strong feelings about your past could be fuel for many positive pursuits in America, even pursuits that could help your country or remaining family.

America – The Second Glance

The initial first glance at America could be called the "honeymoon period." During this period, which could last for many months, you enjoy your travel, meeting with relatives and friends, often being taken care of, finding many things so different and interesting. In spite of any language difficulties and many adjustments, it is similar to a vacation.

This honeymoon period is often the biggest enticement for visitors to stay here. They come on a tourist visa. They get a taste of American life. It is fun, it is new, any old troubles seem so far away, relatives are paying attention to them. The sheer experience of being in a new place makes people feel fresh, alive, involved, important.

But soon reality sets in – the second glance. Probably the second year in America is one of the toughest, emotionally, financially, and physically. By now, the newcomer would have experienced rudeness, would have struggled to find work, would often have put on weight from American food, would have realized the difficulty of trying to communicate without fluency in English, and would have definitely had episodes of loneliness and even depression. The original relationships established in America could become more distant. The anticipations from relatives back home, that instant success can be achieved in America, could create additional pressure.

For many immigrants, the language barrier is naturally very difficult to overcome. But probably the biggest barrier will be psychological. You could truly feel alone here. You have left all your friends, family, the streets that you are accustomed to, the "system" that you know. Everything is different here — customs, traditions, beliefs, behavior. You have to make big changes in the way you think and act.

So what does the newcomer start noticing about America? That some people have a lot, and others are homeless. That, like in their own country, there are good people and bad people. That their relatives or friends who helped them at first, just can't continue to do so. That life in America is not as organized as they thought. In fact, that many things just don't make sense. That there are more questions than answers.

I remember how difficult it was for us when we arrived as refugees in 1972. We thought that there will always be enough money, that if we wanted anything we could get it. In a way, we thought we were special that we escaped, that we were important people, that now someone was going to take care of us, that life will be easy. Well, we were mistaken. We became just like all the other immigrants, working hard to put bread on the table.

In Lithuania, my stepfather was a lawyer and my mother a dermatologist. When they came to America, they made many contacts, had people that helped, and still they could not find good employment for many years. They had to completely start over – new language, new education, new careers. Eventually, they found satisfying work and now they are retired.

My sister, brother, and I also had a difficult time. At school we were teased by American children. We were different, could not speak English well, didn't fit in. We wanted to be like American children, but our parents wanted to keep us like Lithuanian children. With time, we adapted to our new environment, learned English, received good grades in school, made friends. Nothing was easy, however.

The second glance at America could last for many years and could be very discouraging. You may begin to question whether you made the right decision to come here. You may have doubts. This is a dangerous time to make any decisions to go back. Hold off that decision until the third glance.

America – The Third Glance

 "One cannot be an American by going about saying that one is an American. It is necessary to feel America, like America, love America and then work."

— Georgia O'Keeffe.

No country is perfect. But in spite of America's imperfections, it is still one country in the world where an individual can achieve the "impossible." Immigrants have been beating the odds for generations, achieving success despite so many obstacles.

Now, you have also done it. You are here, in America, <u>the land of opportunity</u>. Will you be satisfied with your decision? Satisfied with your new life? I personally know that you can be.

I encourage you to stay excited about America. The following hymn always lifts me up. It was composed in 1893 by Katherine Lee Bates, a Massachusetts educator and author. Its final version was established in 1911.

America, the Beautiful

O beautiful for spacious skies,
For amber waves of grain,
For purple mountain majesties
Above the fruited plain.
America! America!
God shed His grace on thee,
And crown thy good with brotherhood
From sea to shining sea.
O beautiful for pilgrim feet
Whose stern impassioned stress
A thorough-fare for freedom beat
Across the wilderness.
America! America!
God mend thine every flaw,
Confirm thy soul in self control,
Thy liberty in law.

O beautiful for heroes proved
In liberating strife,
Who more than self their country loved
And mercy more than life.
America! America!
May God thy gold refine
Till all success be nobleness,
And every gain divine.
O beautiful for patriot dream
That sees beyond the years,
Thine alabaster cities gleam,
Undimmed by human tears.
America! America!
God shed His grace on thee,
And crown thy good with brotherhood
From sea to shining sea.

According to U.S. Census figures, 25 million people who live in America were not born in America. Nearly one resident in 10 is from another country. In the next 10 years, another 9 million legal immigrants will arrive here. Many will certainly come with ambition, hungry for success, eager to learn, willing to challenge, compete with, and work with Americans. That should not intimidate you, if you prepare adequately.

I would like to close this section with the words of newly-established immigrants from Russia, Vladimir and Dora Ponomareva. Dora says: "...when I wake up every morning I say — thank God I'm here." (Baltimore Sun, 1995.) They have found work, have bought a home, have started a very satisfying new life.

It will certainly not be easy, but the same is very possible for you.

RELATIONSHIPS

Those Strange Americans!

"I've never believed that, to be a part of America, we all have to look alike or dress alike."
—Senator Ben Nighthorse Campbell, Colorado state.

Just reading this book and reflecting on its style can give you a glimpse of American culture. The writing is direct, conversational, oriented to the independent individual. It is concise and gets to the point. It avoids subtleties. It tries to persuade and is meant to save time. That is America in a nutshell! Depending on your cultural beliefs, you may find yourself slightly annoyed.

It is difficult to find a newcomer who will say, "America is exactly how I expected it to be!" While still in their homeland, many have seen American movies and television shows that promote numerous misconceptions about American society. Many come here thinking that everything in America is clean and new, that people are rich without working very hard, that champagne parties are popular, that all houses are modern, that American women are free and easy, and like in the movies, a kid that gets lost in New York could actually check into a luxury hotel. Upon coming here, many are quite surprised.

To make an honest attempt at understanding American culture, it helps to drop all expectations and thus misconceptions. It helps to first accept the fact that <u>most people around the world behave the way they have been taught</u>. (Gary Althen, 1988.) You were taught one way, Americans another way. If you accept this from the very beginning, when you are face-to-face with a confusing cultural situation, it will help you to remain more objective and calm. With luck, you may even meet Americans who accept your behaviors as those handed down to you by your parents and culture.

Let's look at some of the things that newcomers find unsettling about America and its people. Many are confused by American initial friendliness, the smiles, the handshakes, and then the Americans are gone, never to be seen again. They don't understand why many Americans act friendly without actually wanting to become friends. Many come here expecting to develop close friendships with Americans and find out it is difficult. They start labeling an "American smile" as a "phony smile." At least in the beginning, they find America to be a cold and unfriendly place.

It is difficult to generalize about <u>all</u> Americans, because there are so many variations, but let us discuss why, on average, Americans do what they do. First, how do Americans see themselves? Well, most Americans see themselves as friendly and open individuals. They believe that they are <u>separate from others but yet equal</u> (Gary Althen, 1988). Separate because they don't think they belong to any particular group. They want to do their own thing – "I did it my way." Equal because, "everyone is created equal." Most do not regard their behavior as different from anyone else's and many don't think that it is influenced by any specific culture. Even though they see most people as being relatively equal, it does not mean that there isn't wide-spread discrimination in America. It just means that most Americans believe that everyone basically wants similar things in life but they do their own thing to get it.

This separate but equal indoctrination is strange to newcomers. Many cultures emphasize group thinking, following tradition, concern for parental opinions, not being separate. Many look at American separatism as inconsiderate behavior and a lack of concern for other human beings. And some cultures don't view all people as being equal. Some don't view women as being equal to men or they view certain classes of people as superior or inferior.

To Americans time is money. Often it is viewed as even more important than money. Being on time is highly valued and Americans expect this of everyone. In other cultures, time is often not even mentioned. "I'll see you in the evening." When they get there, they get there.

Another cross-cultural difference is that Americans perceive other people in parts, whereas many other cultures perceive a person as a whole (Gary Althen, 1988). Americans will have drinking buddies, shopping buddies, skiing buddies, relaxation buddies, stimulating conversation buddies, business buddies and the list goes on. They build relationships that suit their needs. They find people that like to do the same things. People from other cultures don't see it that way. They see friendships as total commitments. They want to get to know the whole person, to become deeply involved. They don't just want to do surface things, they want to know how people think. They don't understand the American need to always be doing some activity rather than intelligently talking.

Many Americans have trouble just sitting and spending time with other people. They become uncomfortable when no one is speaking. They don't like to argue. They avoid deep subjects such as religion, philosophy or politics. (It doesn't mean they don't <u>think</u> about it. They do. Most just don't talk about it.) They keep conversation on the surface and look for common views. If there is no common view or opinion, often they don't pursue a relationship.

People from other cultures view topics such as politics and religion as the basics of life. They love to talk about deep subjects. That is how they connect with another person. They often view Americans as shallow or not intelligent. "Why do they only talk about sports and the weather?" they ask. Of course, many Americans view the foreigners' attempts at conversation as not very intelligent either. "Why do they get so deep and emotional?"

Another cultural difference is that Americans, for the most part, are concerned more with their future than their past. As you will see in this book, Americans think that they could shape their future by setting goals and striving to achieve them. They think that this could be done by being creative, by working hard, and by improving yourself. Other cultures concentrate on the past more. Ancestry is more important. Some people from these cultures don't think that their fate in the world could truly be changed and that they should accept the life they are given. They want to live passively. Can you see how this could be a problem in America?

Cultural influences start very early in life. Most American families treat their children as small adults. The children's opinions are important. They are given choices. Even from a very young age, they are encouraged to become independent. Their self-esteem is more important then their grades in school. This comes as a surprise for many newcomers. In many other cultures, children are not given choices, they eat what they are given, they are "seen and not heard," their self-esteem is usually tied to academic, athletic or creative accomplishments.

Overall, most Americans honestly believe that America is the best country in the world. And many think that people living in other countries would rather move to America, if given the chance. Because they view America as the best, they view other countries as somehow inferior. This is passed down from generation to generation and reinforced by the floods of immigrants coming in.

You may find many more cultural differences that are not listed here. If there are so many differences and if there are plenty of people from your own country that you can be friends with, why pursue relationships with Americans? It may help to answer this question with the following example. When I spent some time in another country (which I will not specify), I was a foreigner in a strange land. I had a lot of contact with a multinational organization. An ongoing joke among the Americans there was that, trying to reach the local businessmen by phone on a Friday afternoon would be a waste of time, because that was when they were busy making appointments with "concubines". After making an effort to actually get to know the locals, I knew that such a portrayal could never be broadly applied.

If you make the attempt to understand American culture and get to know Americans, you will avoid many misconceptions that are perpetuated by your fellow country-men. You will learn the truth yourself and you will make your own decisions.

■ **Questions**

1. What are some differences between American culture and your country's culture?

2. What do you find most frustrating?

3. What were your expectations about America before you came?

■ ■ ■

Fitting In

 Some newcomers are able to fit into American society better and faster than others. Some may fit in by their profession, but struggle socially outside of work. Dr. Adolfo Lopez, a physician from Venezuela, felt that his profession helped him fit in automatically into the circle of other physicians at the American hospital. But when it came to fitting in with acquaintances outside of work, the language barrier was more detrimental.

To fit in as fast and as best as possible requires that you learn how to communicate in English, that you are sensitive to American-style hygiene and appearance, and that you adopt at least some "American-ized" behaviors. This won't happen overnight.

The first thing to tackle is the English language. If I go to Portugal and I don't speak Portuguese, what are my chances of fitting in with the locals? Slim. The quicker you learn English and can communicate your thoughts and feelings, the quicker you will fit in, make friends, get a job, etc. It is understandable that the first year in America, for the sake of familiarity, assistance and safety, you will stick with people who speak your language. But the sooner you can immerse yourself into English classes, reading English newspapers, magazines, and books, and establishing American relationships, the better for you. This is not to say that you cannot have a satisfying life in your particu-lar ethnic community, speaking primarily your native language. How-ever, without English, your opportunities will be limited in America. It doesn't matter that you speak with an accent or make mistakes. It just matters that you speak, read and write in English. You will begin to fit in as people begin to understand you and feel you understand them.

You have come to America with your own habits and behaviors. They may or may not help you. Through self-examination and observation of Americans around you, you will know which behaviors are suitable. This self-examination is crucial when looking at basic hygiene expectations. While I was living in Lithuania, there was a different concept of hygiene. There was a belief that washing your hair too often would make it fall out. Deodorants were not readily available. Soap and water could not be "wasted" for daily bathing.

In some countries it is quite normal to take a bath and put on the same shirt worn all week. Clothes are often not washed until there is a visible stain on them. In some of these countries, water is scarce and has to be saved. Even upon coming to America, where water and soap are cheap, personal hygiene habits often don't change. What are your beliefs of proper hygiene? Are they different from American beliefs?

Americans, for the most part, are extremely sensitive about odor of any kind, but are especially repelled by body odor. This is reinforced by their upbringing, peers, and television commercials. You will notice that women shave their legs and underarms. Clothing has no particular odors. Teeth are brushed at least twice each day. Hair does not appear oily because it is washed at least a few times a week. Makeup is used sparingly. Most Americans appear clean, without excessive perfumes.

A newcomer who bathes or does his laundry with the same frequency as he did in his own country, may not fit in with Americans. The basic principle of first impressions applies. A first impression is created in the first minute of meeting someone new. It is very difficult to reverse a negative first impression. Someone who emits body odor immediately creates a bad first impression. He may not make that friend or get that job and may never know why. If you want the company of Americans, you need to conform to American standards of hygiene.

Observe what the people around you are doing. What are they wearing? What does their hair look like? How are your kids being treated at school? Are they being teased about anything? Add an extra bath, change undergarments everyday, make sure teeth are brushed. Some ethnic foods stay on a person's breath for two days. It is difficult enough for your children to be "different," you don't want them to also be "avoided."

Speaking of teeth, they are a big deal for most Americans. In no other country is so much value placed on straight, white, clean teeth. Obviously, Americans don't think highly of gold teeth. Even if you do everything else right, your visible gold tooth will always stand out. If you are from a country that used gold caps to repair front teeth, you may want to consider visiting a good dentist for an evaluation. (One low-cost option would be the dental school of a local university.)

Newcomers often remark that Americans dress sloppy. Comfort is very important but certain rules are usually followed. When my cousin from Lithuania came for a visit, he could not understand why I asked him not to wear black socks with his white sports shoes. Well, Americans just don't do that. If you want to fit in, really observe what the people around you are wearing. You will see that they don't wear the same clothes two days in a row. In every other country that I have ever visited, this is quite normal. If you observe carefully, you will notice that the colors and materials of the clothes are coordinated. You could have the cleanest hygiene, speak English fluently, yet immediately be spotted as a foreigner depending on the clothes you put on.

If you have already analyzed your learned behaviors and habits, which have a strong cultural basis, you will know which ones need work. For example, if you brought with you a belief that to be taken seriously in business, you have to be cold and tough, avoid smiling, try to win so the other guy loses, you will find that this attitude will probably not work in America. It is not based on courtesy, friendliness, or openness. Or, if you are used to giving a soft handshake with your eyes lowered, as is the custom in some cultures, you may want to "Americanize" it somewhat. Americans expect eye contact, a smile, and a firm, quick handshake. Or, if you are always late for meetings and social events, because it didn't matter in your country, it will matter here.

When dealing with American companies or institutions, it is best to follow the expected procedures. American bureaucracy has a certain process and takes time. Ask what that process is and what you need to do. In some countries, you need to go to the boss to get anything done. Not necessarily so in America. Lower level employees can usually handle most things. Fitting in often requires working "the system" with courtesy and patience.

There is one obstacle to your fitting in that I have not mentioned yet, which you will undoubtedly experience. It is xenophobia. This is a big word to basically describe "a fear of anything strange or foreign." That is usually not your problem. It is the other person's problem. If you have made an honest effort to fit in, you have done your part. Again, this requires that you learn how to communicate in English, that you are sensitive to American-style hygiene and appearance, and that you adopt at least some "Americanized" behaviors. Armed with these basics, you are prepared to get to know Americans and for them to get to know you.

■ Questions

1. What efforts are recommended to help the process of fitting in?
2. What efforts would be required of foreigners in your country?

■ ■ ■

Start First and Go Slowly

"Americans won't talk to me!" This is a common complaint from new immigrants. A good response would be, "When you were in your country, did you strike up many conversations with foreigners?" The answer will probably be "no."

If you want to start a friendship or some connection with an American, you will have to start talking first and you will have to build the friendship slowly. You will have to start first for the same reason why a foreigner in your country would have to start first to get to know you. Most people, in most countries, do not try to find foreigners with whom they could develop relationships. It is a common universal attitude. It doesn't mean they don't want to be friends with foreigners. It just means that they will wait for the foreigner to start first. So, you as a foreigner in America, need to take that first step.

It is not difficult to start talking to Americans. If you are nervous, it is alright to say so. If the room is too hot, start with that. Ask about anything. Ask about their families, their jobs, hobbies, travel experiences, even ask about cultural factors. Just don't start with any topics about money, religion, philosophy or politics. Showing a sincere interest in the other person is the best strategy. Say a little about yourself and get the other person to talk. The more the other person talks, the better chance you will see him again.

Avoid becoming a "time thief." Nothing creates an impression of selfishness or boredom more than a person who talks too much or stays too long. Show control by knowing when to close a conversation. Don't wait for the other person to say they have to go. Time is valuable for everyone. Politely excuse yourself and allow the person to meet others. If it is someone you would be interested in seeing again, ask the person what would be the best way to "get a hold" of him or her. They may give you their business card or home number or ask you for yours.

With Americans you need to go slowly. If you unload your whole life story, share all your problems, brag about all your accomplishments, dig too deeply for stimulating conversation trying to get to know the "real" person, you will scare most Americans away. Again, remember what an individualistic, independent person would do. He obviously would be frightened away by anyone dependent and clingy.

Also, remember that Americans like to always be doing something. Try the approach of "let's go shopping together," or "I rented a video, do you want to come over to watch it?" Concentrate at first on <u>doing</u> rather than <u>knowing</u>. In some countries, friendships are established to value <u>differences</u> between people, so people can learn from one another. In America it is the opposite. Friendships are established according to <u>similarities</u>. "The more you are like me, the better chance we will become friends."

As a general guideline, if you smoke, be sensitive to where you do it. It is best to smoke only when someone else is already smoking. Even when your opinion is asked, don't criticize America or its political system. It is funny that the Americans themselves feel free to do it, but they don't want foreigners to do it. If you are a male, don't stand too close or touch an American male. Most will react very negatively. And most of all, don't judge what is right or wrong in most situations. You will be applying your own cultural thinking and you are no longer in your own culture.

There are many things that you may feel are strange about America or the new relationships you start to develop. If you can hold off judging and take the time to listen, learn, and understand, you may see things from a different angle.

▪ Questions

1. How do you feel about initiating a conversation with an American?
2. What are some good topics of discussion?
3. What are some activities that you and an American friend can do together?

▪ ▪ ▪

Relationship Fundamentals

 The universally-applicable fundamentals of building relationships include trusting others, being honest, noticing the good that others do, being kind, and apologizing when you make a mistake. It could be summed up by one word – respect. If you do the fundamentals with people, you show them respect. No matter what country, no matter what culture. If you respect others, they are more likely to respect you. Let us look at the fundamentals briefly.

Trust people from the first time you meet them, even if you know they may not trust you. It sounds ridiculous, but try. Trust is the one essential ingredient in any relationship. And it has to start with someone. If you simply expect good behavior from the people you meet, they will sense it and most likely not disappoint you. You can experiment with this. With the next two new people you meet, trust one and don't trust the other. See which one is easier to talk to, which person is more fun, which person you are more likely to see again.

Be honest in your dealings with other people. You may fool them once, but probably not twice. People can usually detect dishonest behavior and speech. Keep the agreements you make. Breaking agreements not only damages relationships with others but it also damages your self-respect. You will not be able to trust your own word.

Too often we try to watch for other people's faults and mistakes. And, of course, we always find some because nobody is perfect. And then we say, "aha, I knew he would disappoint me." Remember, most people want to do the right thing. Instead of wasting energy waiting for mistakes to happen, notice the good things that people do.

Kindness should be utilized not only for friends and family, but for the waitress who serves you coffee, for the man who cuts your hair, for the person who sits next to you on the bus, and for every person who passes through your life. A person who treats each relationship as valuable will probably respond to most of the advice in this section with "of course, it's only common sense!" Knowing and willing to treat others with respect, by doing the fundamentals, is half the battle to a successful life, in America or anywhere.

■ Question

1. What are some universal relationship fundamentals?

■ ■ ■

Four Social Styles

"When enthusiasm is inspired by reason, controlled by caution, and practical in application, it reflects confidence, inspires associates, and arouses loyalty." — Coleman Cox.

To effectively communicate, it helps to know the other person's frame of reference, culture, and tradition. Many misunderstandings occur because what is acceptable for some people is unacceptable for others. For example, in America, hosts do not keep offering more food to their guests, convincing them to keep eating. According to Lithuanian tradition this is expected. In Japan, when you are given someone's business card, it is like receiving a photo of the person. You must look at it carefully with respect before putting it in your pocket. In America, you can just stick it in your pocket.

In America you will face a large variety of people with varied cultural backgrounds. You will certainly spend some time trying to figure them out. No doubt, you will be confused. In language study there is a term called "chunking," learning parts of words and phrases. It may help to do that also with people. "Chunk" them according to their social style. It will help you to respond to them more appropriately, at least until you understand them more fully.

Each person tends to adopt a particular social style when dealing with others. The style a person adopts becomes difficult to change. If we know other people's style, we can somewhat predict their likes and dislikes. We get an idea of how they are likely to respond to events in their lives. We become more effective in reaching our goals with people. Four types of social styles will be described. They are based on the notable Wilson Learning System. Which style are your friends? Which one is your boss? Which one are you married to? Which one are you?

The four social styles are: driver, expressive, amiable, and analytical. Some people have a combination of two styles, but generally one style predominates and is the most noticeable. You will sense a person's style from the first few sentences he says and the way he behaves.

A driver style values results and likes to be in control. In dealing with these types of people, it is best to be prepared so you are efficient and don't waste their time. Be formal and direct, listen carefully. Give them options and support their conclusions. If confronted or under stress, drivers may become autocratic and refuse to compromise. If you are a driver yourself, you can develop your people skills by listening more to other people. What are they saying? What are they feeling? Are they being reasonable?

An expressive style values recognition and likes to be social. With these types of people, it helps to be mentally stimulating. Share stories, don't rush discussions, appreciate their humor. In confrontational situations, expressives will tend to attack back. If you are an expressive, you can develop your people skills by stopping and checking to see how people are doing. Are they bored, happy, hurried, tired, angry? Have you said enough for now?

An amiable style values attention and likes to be supportive. These types of people love agreement and compromise. They like assurances and to keep relationships. Show them your personal commitment, share your feelings, don't push, be patient. If confronted, amiables will generally appear to give in. They will agree with what you say, but will do the opposite. If you are an amiable yourself, the way to develop your people skills is to initiate conversations and action more often. Don't wait for the other person to do it first.

An analytical style values specifics and likes to be technical. In dealing with these types, it is a good idea to provide accurate details whenever possible. They need to see evidence and must have time to think. Ask for their advice, avoid being emotional, stay organized. When confronted, analyticals will try to avoid the situation. They will find a way to excuse themselves. If you are an analytical, you can develop your people skills by making decisions after you receive a reasonable amount of information. Don't keep digging for more and more details never quite reaching a decision. This is very frustrating for other people. There comes a point when the information you have is enough.

As you see, a common theme with all of the above is that, if you want something from someone else, confrontation probably won't work. No matter what your social style or the other person's social style, quiet confidence and enthusiasm will help. Be prepared, confident, and enthusiastic. Have a few intelligent questions in mind. Let them talk more. Make them feel special. Your understanding of where they are coming from and your non-judgmental attitude will surprise and relax them. If you understand them, they stand a better chance of understanding and accepting you.

■ **Questions**

1. What are the four basic social styles?
2. Which one are you?

How Men and Women Communicate

Humor break:

A woman was walking her dog in the park.

"What a beautiful puppy," remarked Peter, who was actually more interested in the young lady. "Does he have a genealogical tree?"

"Uh... yes," blushed the lady, "as soon as you enter the park, the second one to the right."

Whether in business or at home, men and women communicate differently. For the most part, they simply think differently. You will find this to be true for many different cultures. This section is based on the writings of Deborah Tannen, a linguistics specialist and an expert in male and female communication styles.

Generally speaking, most men base their communication on the judgment of whether they are in an <u>up</u> or <u>down</u> position. Women, on the other hand, base their communication on the judgment of whether they will be <u>closer</u> to the person they are speaking with or <u>further away</u>. Following are some examples.

Most men have difficulty asking for directions when they get lost because that would put them in a <u>down</u> position, admitting that they are lost. They would much rather drive around until they find where they are going or have the woman ask for help. For women to ask for directions seems like an easy task. They don't see it as <u>up</u> or <u>down</u> and may become annoyed that the men don't take charge and get directions themselves. Often, that is how confusion and disagreements start in relationships. One side does not see where the other side is coming from.

As another example, say a wife comes home after a difficult day at work and starts to share the bad situation with her husband. She wants to get <u>closer</u> to him. She just wants him to listen and be there. The husband, however, starts to give the wife advice on how he would have handled the problem. It is his opportunity to help, to be <u>up</u>. Well, the last thing she wants is advice because that pushes her <u>further away</u>. She wouldn't solve the problem the way he would and now she feels different from him. He becomes annoyed that she doesn't listen to his advice and puts him in a <u>down</u> position. She becomes annoyed that he doesn't get <u>closer</u>. Another misunderstanding.

If the story is reversed and the husband had the bad day, it could again cause trouble. He would come home and not readily admit that he had a bad day, especially if the wife had a good one, because that would put him in a <u>down</u> position. The wife, sensing that something is wrong, would start questioning and showing concern, her attempt at getting <u>closer</u>. Well, that would only make him feel more <u>down</u>. He may tell her to leave him alone. For no good reason, an argument can start.

In business, the misunderstandings could occur in the way men and women perceive one another. Because women communicate to move <u>closer</u>, they seek more to understand, rather than to be understood. They tend to ask more questions, seek clarifications, and enjoy small talk. Men may mistakenly perceive them as nosy and weak.

Men, as we have seen, communicate with different goals. Because they want to be in an <u>up</u> position, they seek more to be understood. They prefer to state their opinions, interrupt others, provide instructions, and enjoy competitive discussions. Women may mistakenly perceive them as overly aggressive and insensitive.

As with cross-cultural understanding, appreciating the basic differences in male/female communication styles could be a relief for couples at home and for colleagues at work. It is no use trying to change each other. By appreciating the differences, perceptions could be more realistic and many misunderstandings could be avoided. The more we understand each other, the better we work together, the better we live together, and the more we enjoy each other's company.

■ Questions

1. What are some basic communication style differences between men and women?
2. How do they compare to the communication styles in your country?

Our Feelings are Hard to Hide

 "Anything in life that we don't accept will simply make trouble for us until we make peace with it." — Shakti Gawain.

In everything we do, we communicate to other people what we feel. We cannot hide it. Our feelings will always betray us. Consider the following story. There was a man who was in charge of group training at a large organization. One winter he was in an auto accident and lost his left arm. He had a great deal of difficulty coping with his loss. During the next three years, he trained thirty groups. Never, during those three years, did a single person ask him about his arm.

Then, through some professional counseling, this man came to a personal resolution and finally accepted the loss of his arm. He decided that, despite his misfortune, his life was good and he had so much to offer to others. Over the next three years he trained thirty more groups and there was never a time that someone within the group not ask him about his arm. In some unconscious way, before he accepted his fate, he was sending out a message through his behavior, "do not ask me about my arm, I am ashamed of it, it's none of your business." When he made peace with himself, he became approachable and friendly.

Another example of a feeling that is hard to hide is when someone feels superior to us. Isn't that just obvious? It will be in their voice, their mannerism, their posture, their language. The same goes when someone feels inferior, angry, envious, or any other strong emotion. Feelings will peek through like mushrooms after a rainstorm. It is no use trying to hide them.

There may be some people who say, "well, I want people to know that I'm smarter and better than them." This is simply not logical and totally self-destructive. For the best outcome, in any situation, you do not want to appear better than the person you are interacting with. You may be more educated, have more money, be more popular, it does not matter. To protect their own feelings, people will simply not see you that way. They will see you as arrogant, annoying, and pompous. This is not a good start for any relationship. Always remember that it is always best to be perceived as likable, warm, and friendly.

Since it is so difficult to hide what we truly feel, don't even try. It is easier to simply change what you feel. Finding something that you like about the other person is the easiest and most effective way to change how you feel. Notice that I am not recommending that you pretend to like someone. If you look hard enough, you will always find something real to like. Pretending to like someone hurts your integrity and will be visible to everyone.

Keep in mind that 90% of effective communication comes from <u>how</u> one communicates, only 10% from what the person actually says. If you are self-conscious about your accent, for example, you will come across less confident and your accent will become even more noticeable. Talk with your accent, make mistakes, but talk with confidence.

■ Questions

1. How do our feelings affect our behavior?
2. How can we control our feelings for the best communication results?

■ ■ ■

Getting Your Point Across

"Words have no meaning if you utter them carelessly… nobody will ever understand you, if you are afraid to say what you want…" — song clip, Foje.

As you have seen, different social styles and gender require different communication strategies. So what happens when it is time for you to get your specific point across? You may need to establish a contact, state your position, describe your idea or product, sell something, or simply communicate effectively in social situations.

The key to effective communication, when your message must be heard and understood, is this: when it comes time to make your main point, make it direct, clear, and make it in less than 30 seconds. (Frank O. Milo, 1986.) That is not much time, but if you talk at length <u>around</u> the main point, the listener may lose your overall message. All immigrants from cultures that emphasize subtlety, indirect conversation, endless descriptions, please read this section three times.

We live in a "sound-bite" world. We remember bits and pieces of what we hear. We sum things up in one phrase. Television and radio commercials are aware of people's short attention spans. They try to form impressions using just the right few words.

So much communication gets lost, when people are not forward and direct. So, even if you have 10 minutes, 30 minutes, or 2 hours, make your main point in less than 30 seconds. And keep in mind that people who talk less are listened to more. What captures your attention better, the constant ticking of the clock or the ringing telephone?

■ Questions

1. Why is it important to get to the point?
2. Are you accustomed to talking directly and clearly?

■　■　■

A Friend of a Friend

"Nothing is impossible for the man who doesn't have to do it himself." — A.H. Weiler.

 As you go through your life, you will meet a lot of people. You never know how important these people may become for you. Counting relatives, business associates, friends, and friends of friends, each person creates a network of 250 to 1000 acquaintances. If you create a bad impression about yourself or break off a relationship in a negative manner, you have lost not one person, but many.

It is very difficult to find success without some assistance from other people. The trouble is you never know which of the people you meet will actually help you on the way to success. The best policy is to know as many people as possible. Not everyone has to be good friends of yours. They just have to be acquaintances that have a good impression of you.

I used to work with a man that I would call a champion networker. He knows so many people. He sends out hundreds of Christmas and birthday cards every year. He can travel practically anywhere in the U.S. and have a free place to spend the night. He knows how to buy the best things for the best price, because he knows whom to call. He will never be without a job. He will never be without a friend.

Build a network of contacts in America. Don't dismiss anyone too easily. You never know where a certain relationship can go. But always keep in mind the popular proverb: "Tell me whom you frequent, and I will tell you who you are." Know a lot of people, but pick your closest friends carefully.

■ Questions

1. Do you have a plan for networking?
2. Where do you meet most people and how do you keep in touch with them?

■ ■ ■

Conflict Management

"If two friends ask you to judge a dispute, don't accept, because you will lose one friend; on the other hand, if two strangers come with the same request, accept, because you will gain one friend." — Saint Augustine.

Whenever two people spend time together, sooner or later, conflict will occur. Managing conflict comes down to managing your words. Words could be as gentle as rose petals or as deadly as knives. The words you choose to use will determine whether you will be effective in conflict management and thus effective in maintaining relationships. What is the use of making relationships if you can't maintain them?

In any interaction with another person, you have your agenda. The person you are interacting with also has his agenda. How you respond to each other's agenda will either result in a smooth interaction or a conflicting one.

Some people internalize angry feelings, if someone irritates them. Others become rude and try to hurt the other person. This often causes the death of many relationships. People who refuse other points of view, who refuse to budge from their own agenda, who are inflexible, will probably make poor communicators and poor friends.

If you want permanent, healthy relationships, practice talking honestly about your feelings, without attacking the dignity of the other person. You don't have to agree with people or give in. But it is very beneficial to you to remain fair, civil, and kind. Don't think that for you to gain something, someone else has to give up something. Think that both of you can win and you will find a compromise.

■ Questions

1. How are you used to resolving conflicts?
2. Is there room for improvement?

EDUCATION

Life-Long Learning

 "Each day I learn more than I teach ...I learn that what we expect we get...I learn that there's more good than evil in this world... I learn how much there is to learn." — Virginia Church.

Education will always take top priority in America. Making a commitment to life-long learning is an important habit of success. We must invest in ourselves and develop our skills, regardless of our age, background, or country of origin.

As you work toward achieving your goals in America, determine your strengths and weaknesses. List them on a piece of paper. Weaknesses that interfere with your goals need to be overcome through experience and learning. There is not enough time to learn everything possible. <u>Time, money and energy should be invested to learn the things necessary to reach your goals</u>.

Success will always require knowledge and work. It is like cultivating a garden. You must have a plan, prepare the soil, plant the seeds, water regularly, protect from insects, pull the weeds. It doesn't happen overnight. You may fail at times, but usually, what you put in, you get back.

Here's an illustration of how learning effects our lives as it strengthens our minds. It relates to the children's story about the three little pigs. The person who has built his mind out of straw will cave in under the slightest pressure. The person whose mind is built out of wood has enough mental strength to withstand a fair amount of pressure, adversity, and uncertainty. The person whose mind is built out of bricks has the knowledge, experience, direction, and determination to meet most challenges in life. (I think I am at the wood stage. Where are you?)

In this land of opportunity, let education expand your curiosity and openness to new people, new ideas and new possibilities.

■ Questions

1. What are your strengths and weaknesses?
2. What do you need to learn to reach your goals in America?

■ ■ ■

English, English, English

 "The only thing newcomers need is good English. Yes, of course, people need to eat something and stay somewhere, but without English they won't be able to reach the American Dream." Those are the words of Leonid A. Shraybman, who is originally from Ukraine. The young man arrived to Baltimore to rejoin his family. Demonstrating good English and strong computer skills, he found work and continues his studies. He is looking forward to becoming a U.S. citizen.

To obtain citizenship, you will need to show a competency of English. You will need to learn how to read it, write it, and pass an examination about U.S. history. Don't look for shortcuts. Immigrants who minimize learning English, will minimize the quality of their life in America. A study of Southeast Asian refugees found that those who spoke English fluently earned almost three times more money than those who did not. (Reader's Digest, 1996.) This, no doubt, applies to newcomers from all over the world.

Sometimes newcomers want to learn just enough English to "get by," to survive. They don't plan to stay in America forever. They take an English class for a few months, learn a few sentences, get a job and quit studying. Even if you decide to go back to your country, why not make studying English as one of your daily top priorities while you are here? If you learn it well, won't it be a valuable skill if you decide to go back? Why not learn to speak, read and write the most popular language in the world?

When we first came over, my sister and I attended 5th grade in a bilingual elementary school in Chicago. The school taught classes in English and Lithuanian. It provided a good transition period for us in our first year in America. But when we moved to Virginia the following year, we attended a regular American school. It was more stressful but we learned English faster. Decide what is best for you and your children for the first year or two, but after that, immerse yourself and your children in total English.

An excellent way to learn English is in a classroom. Take an English to Speakers of Other Languages (ESOL or ESL) class and stick with it. Classes are available throughout America, in cities and suburbs. Every morning during breakfast pick a new word from the dictionary and learn it together with your family. Talk to yourself in English as you are doing things around the house. Watch educational programs on television. Listen to National Public Radio. (Available throughout the U.S. Listen especially to the Diane Rehm show, Monday through Friday, from 10:00am - 12:00pm and again at 9:00pm Eastern time. It is not only an informative program, but she speaks using very deliberate, articulate words.) Listen to English language tapes. Repeat things out loud. Carry your dictionary with you. Do not let an opportunity slip by to look up a new word or communicate with a potential new friend.

■ **Questions**

1. How many hours do you spend every day studying or talking in English?
2. What else can you do to learn correct English faster?

The Land of Computers

 In your search to learn as much as possible, keep in mind that in the U.S., profits come more from the exchange of data, information, and knowledge rather than the production of goods. (Robert B. Reich, 1992.) Worldwide, this exchange of knowledge is usually communicated using computers. You will need to get comfortable with them, no matter what your age. You will need a computer to learn, you will need it for work, you will need it for your kids, you will need it to remain competitive.

If you already know a lot about computers, congratulations! It is such a valuable skill. If you don't know how to use computers, don't get discouraged. Powerful computers are becoming less expensive and easier to use. Many people know how to use them. You are sure to find someone that can help you get started. If not, computer training classes are widely available. Community colleges offer a variety of them. Pick up a course catalog at your local library.

■ Internet

If you are new to the world of computers, words like "Internet," "information superhighway," "Net surfing," "World Wide Web," and many others could sound confusing. Again, don't get discouraged. And, especially, <u>don't ignore it</u>.

What is the Internet and why do you need it? Isn't it funny that just a few years ago, people asked "what is a fax machine and why do you need it?" Without getting into too much technical language, the Internet is a world-wide network of computers. Just imagine thousands and thousands of computers somehow connected. In front of each of those computers is a human being. Subscribing to the Internet, is like joining a club with thousands of members. You can communicate with them using your computer, writing letters called E-mail (electronic mail). E-mail messages are fast, efficient, and best of all, <u>free</u>. With the click of a button you can send your message to one person or to hundreds of people.

Internet users have varied personalities, information, ideas, experience. They are government agencies, corporations, small businesses, educational institutions, and regular folks like you and me. Announcements on the Internet can be to sell something, to list a job opening, to inform, to warn, or for any other agenda. No one is in charge of the Internet or the quality of its information. Just as somebody can send good and bad information on a fax machine, the same applies to the Internet. You have to be the judge.

As a newcomer, you will probably use the Internet to search for information and to communicate with other people, maybe with others from your country. If you have a particular hobby, there are people with similar interests that would love to communicate with you. You can use the Internet to learn more about America, about the changing immigration policies, about jobs that are available, about college application procedures, about traveling, about anything that affects your life.

If you have your own computer or have access to one through a family member or friend, consider subscribing to an <u>online service</u>. Look through computer magazines in the library for comparisons of different online service providers. As you call around, ask what the <u>local dial-up number</u> would be to make sure it is not a long distance call for you.

One of the least expensive ways is to sign up through your local library. It may cost anywhere from $50 to $100 per year for unlimited access to the Internet. You may experience more busy signals than with commercial services. For some libraries, you would still need to use your own computer and just dial into the library system. At other libraries, computers are available specifically for the Internet and can be used by the general public. Check around. Whatever service you choose, make sure it gives you unlimited access for a monthly fee. Some services charge you a monthly fee and an hourly rate.

This book makes it easy for you to get started on the Internet. Use the locations (the "http" addresses) in the section called **Sampling the Internet** in the **Appendix**, to look up additional information, to find help, to search what is available on any topic. If you are using a computer at school or work, someone there can probably help you log on and type in your first search address. From there, you can figure it out on your own. If you are still shy about it, consider taking an Internet training class. They are offered by many community colleges, at computer learning centers, Internet service providers, and many private organizations. For computer hardware and software suggestions that make Internet access possible, see the section called **Major Purchases**.

■ Questions

1. What information would you look for on the Internet?
2. How comfortable are you with computers?

■ ■ ■

College Education

Humor break:
"Sound really does travel slower than light. The advice parents give to their 18-year-olds doesn't reach them until they're about 40." — *Orben's Current Comedy.*

■ Getting In

 Before hurrying to get accepted into a college, reflect on your goals. College may not be the answer for everyone. There are also various other paths a person can take. There are vocational schools that provide medical training, such as physical therapy, business training, such as accounting, and technical training, such as computer programming. These schools offer day and evening classes, are less expensive than a four-year college degree, and are easier to get into. They also provide assistance in getting work after you graduate.

Community colleges offer two-year programs. Many are excellent choices for students. Some students get a two-year degree called an Associate of Arts (AA) and then transfer to a four-year college to get a Bachelor of Arts (BA) or a Bachelor of Science (BS). Many of the credits are transferable. Community colleges are less expensive and you can find one close to home. And they are less likely to be taught by Teacher's Assistants (TA's), which is common at four-year colleges.

Colleges look at various areas of student performance before accepting them. They look at the Scholastic Assessment Test (SAT) results, high school grades, where the student ranks in comparison to fellow classmates, and what activities the student was involved in during the high school years (called extracurricular activities). If English is not your native language, you will also have to take the Test of English as a Foreign Language (TOEFL). The academic records and other degrees from your country will probably need to be translated, if they are not in English. For information call the World Education Services, Inc., ☎1-212-966-6311.

The SAT is taken by a million high school students every year. It is the most widely used college entrance exam. It tests mathematical, verbal, and reasoning skills. The better score you get, the more choices of colleges you will have. There are SAT preparation classes that you can take, but they are expensive (about $500-$700 for 36 hours). The most popular companies that offer them are: Princeton Review, Sylvan Learning Centers, and Kaplan Educational Centers, Inc. High schools and community colleges may offer similar courses at a lower cost. The average math and verbal combined SAT score is about 900 (out of a possible 1600). To get into certain colleges, you will need much higher than average.

If you can show good SAT scores, some challenging activities in high school, and good high school grades, getting into a college you want should not be difficult. All that is left is the application process. Most college applications contain some standard questions and ask you to write an essay (for example, a few paragraphs about a particular achievement).

To learn how America ranks its best colleges and universities, go to the library and find the *U.S. News & World Report's* issue that ranks them. This magazine is highly respected and rates colleges every year. They look at college size, geographical location, educational focus, reputation, professor qualifications, student satisfaction.

You will be the best judge as to which college is right for you. If you start early, in your junior year of high school, you will have time to visit the colleges you are considering. Call the admissions officer to find out what you are able to see during your visit. Some can even arrange an overnight stay at a dormitory so you can get a taste of college life.

■ **Paying For It**

Getting into college can be challenging. Paying for it can be brutal. Most people pay for college using a combination of personal savings, grants, and loans. The earlier you start to save for college, the better. As is discussed in the **Money** section, you can save for college using some basic investment principles: starting early, investing a set amount every month, vowing to never touch the money until college time.

Private colleges are usually the most expensive. Adding up tuition, fees, housing, meals, books, and miscellaneous expenses, it could cost about $20,000 per school year. <u>Don't let the lack of money keep you from applying to the best schools</u>. Private colleges offer many scholarships and discounts. If they want you, they will make you a nice offer. Show them what other colleges are offering and negotiate for even more. (For a short list of good colleges at reasonable prices, see the **Appendix**.)

State universities are less expensive, about $10,000 per year. Many state universities provide a quality education, for the best price, <u>if you are a resident of the state</u>. To be considered a resident, you usually have to prove that you lived in the state for at least one year before the first semester starts. State universities are more likely to give financial aid to students within their state.

Whatever option you choose, it will still be expensive. Many people apply for financial aid. The federal government funds the Pell Grant and the Supplemental Education Opportunity Grant (SEOG). This money does not have to be repaid. A lot of it is available and is awarded according to a family's need. Education loans are also widely available, but have to be repaid with interest. The Federal Perkins Loan has the lowest interest rate (about 5%). Most education loans don't require repayment until after you graduate from college. Also available are work-study programs. To see what programs are being offered, you can contact the Financial Aid Administrator's Office at the colleges you are considering. Some information may also be provided by your high school. Check into it in your senior year. The library also has publications about all sorts of financial aid.

You will have to apply for aid for each college year. Two important things — complete the necessary forms fully and submit them early. Mark your calendar with all the deadline dates. Keep an organized folder of all applications and information. Make copies of everything that will leave your hands. Papers could get lost. Your high school should provide a *Free Application for Federal Student Aid* (FAFSA). Or you can get one sent to you by calling, ☎1-800-4-FED-AID (1-800-433-3243). (If you get aid in the first year, you will need to continue submitting a *Renewal FAFSA*, a shorter form.) Send the clean, fully-completed, signed FAFSA to the address indicated on the form, on or after January 1 of the year you plan to attend.

After about a month, you will receive a *Student Aid Report* (SAR). The SAR will show how much your family is expected to contribute toward college expenses. Make copies of the SAR and mail them to the colleges you have chosen. The colleges that accept you will send you a financial aid award letter. The letter will state what each college plans to give you. Any numbers listed under a loan category are not automatic. You have to apply for them separately. Call SallieMae's College Answer Service, at ☎1-800-222-7183. They can provide more information on financial aid programs and the application process.

My first year in college, I obtained very little financial aid, when my parents' income was considered. But when I started working part-time and left home, my parents did not claim me as a dependent on their tax returns. I was able to obtain much more financial aid in the following years, because only my own income was considered.

However, if you plan to continue living at home, it is better to have most of the savings and investment accounts in your parent's name. Financial aid officers consider that about 5% of your parent's savings should go toward your college expenses. If the money is in your name, they expect 35-50%. They subtract these numbers out before making you eligible for financial aid. Note: You want the tax return from December of the junior year in high school to January of the senior year to look as poor as possible, if you want financial aid. This means, you don't cash out pension plans, IRAs, sell stocks, etc., during this period. It will show up as extra cash and you don't want that.

Students with athletic talents may be able to get into a good university easier and find financial support more available. Athletic scholarships are especially becoming more available for women. Notre Dame, for example, awards $22,600 to cover tuition and room and board (living expenses) to women volleyball players (Reader's Digest,

1996). There are scholarship funds available for almost every sport. Some universities also try to attract talents in music, theater, and art. Whatever talents you have, see if there is a scholarship offered for it.

You may also consider applying to the AmeriCorps organization. It offers over 350 programs nationwide and works a lot like the Peace Corps. Someone who is accepted in one of the programs, for example, in the Habitat for Humanity program, will receive educational credits that could be applied to future tuition costs. They may also receive some wages, health coverage, and other benefits. Call AmeriCorps for more information and an application form, ☎1-800-942-2677. All U.S. citizens and permanent residents age 17 and older are eligible to apply.

■ Note to Parents

Your children's education is most likely a top priority. It may be one of the main reasons you came to America. However, always keep in mind that your first priority should be saving money for your own retirement. Once you have a monthly plan for your own retirement savings, work on saving for your children's college expenses. Don't use your retirement money to pay for college. It is a mistake many parents make.

If you have your own business, as many foreign-born Americans do, a great way to grow money for college expenses is to hire your own children. Unlike regular employers, parents can hire their children at any age. You can assign some specific part-time duties, such as stuffing envelopes, passing out fliers, running errands, cleaning, etc. You can then invest their earned income under their names in a tax-deferred Individual Retirement Account (IRA) stock mutual fund. IRA's can only be funded from earned income.

The earlier your son or daughter earns money and invests it, the greater the interest compounding will be. Money in an IRA is not considered by college financial aid officers, so it won't hurt their eligibility for aid. If financial aid is scarce at the time they apply, the IRA is available. Under the new Roth IRA, you may withdraw money for qualified higher education expenses without having to pay a penalty. And if your children won't need to withdraw the money until they retire, they will be financially ahead of most retirees in America. See the section on **Money** for more details about IRA's.

■ Making the Most of Your College Years

"A college education should equip one to entertain three things: a friend, an idea and oneself."
— Thomas Ehrlich.

<u>If you work at it</u>, your college education could prepare you for a meaningful career. Unfortunately, many students, foreign and American, are either too swept up with academics or the social life to really reflect on what would make a suitable career for them. So to "work at it" really means to get the most out of what college has to offer.

<u>To be an attractive candidate for many employers, college grades will not be as important as the actual learning, internships, clubs, jobs, and other extracurricular activities you can show</u>. Unless you are pursuing a highly specialized field, such as medicine, getting good grades and doing little of anything else will not be enough in this competitive marketplace. Most companies would rather see a 3.0 average and high involvement in other activities, than a 3.9 average with no involvement. However, as was already mentioned, <u>high school grades and good SAT scores are important</u> to get into a good college and to help obtain financial aid. So worry more about high school grades than college grades.

The employment world is rapidly changing. A person who thinks that he or she could study to become an engineer, could get a job as an engineer, and could retire as the same engineer is being unrealistic. In the current job market, most people will work 5 to 10 different jobs before retiring. So, choosing a major is not like choosing someone you will marry. You don't have to spend your whole life with your decision. Most people don't. Major in what you want to learn about the most and add classes that teach you some business basics, such as making presentations, writing business letters, using computers. Don't worry if you jump from the Art Club to the Science Club, and then drop both to take up weightlifting. That's what college is all about. The time to get worried is when there is no action — if all you do is study all day and watch television all night.

The purpose of going to college is to discover what it is that we enjoy doing. Many people overlook that. If you graduate without knowing what you would enjoy doing for a living, you may end up doing what you hate. Don't most people that you would consider successful actually enjoy their work?

In some countries, parents are expected to recommend and influence what their children will pursue as their life-long work. Why this needs to be a personal choice, especially in America, is quite evident in today's job market. The people who are most successful are the ones that persist in their work inspite of obstacles. It is hard to persist and produce good results if you hate your job. If you came to America to improve your quality of life, why don't you pursue a career that will give you the most personal satisfaction?

The best way to choose work you will love to do, and thus the most appropriate major, start looking at how you feel about your various classes. Which books interest you the most? Which magazines catch your eye? What activity makes the time fly by quickly? Whose life do you envy? Walk through the public library and look at the subject headings posted — psychology, history, home improvement, management, animals, etc. Which headings make you want to stop and browse. If you are interested in a couple of subjects, think how they may combine. For example, the subjects of psychology, art, and business would always capture my attention. Writing books makes use of all the topics I love, from doing the research, creating the product, and developing a marketing plan.

Each semester try to arrange your classes so that you have large blocks of time open. Many semesters I was able to arrange my schedule so that I didn't have any classes on Tuesdays and Thursdays. Make time available for an internship. Get a part-time job. Do volunteer work. Get involved in various clubs. Don't just concentrate all your attention on your class work or social life.

Inquire at your college about opportunities to spend a semester overseas (in an English-speaking country if English is still your weak point). In my sophomore year, I spent part of the summer in Madrid, Spain. I took a comprehensive Spanish course and lived with a Spanish family. It was an incredible experience and always looks good on my resume.

Call the Council on International Educational Exchange (CIEE) at ☎1-212-822-2600 and ask them to send you some information on studying in the country of your interest. Also ask about the International Student Identity Card and information about finding summer jobs abroad.

Keep in mind that, academics is not real life. In real life you will need to think, to lead, to make effective decisions, and to sell yourself. Most textbooks don't teach that. You will need to seek out opportunities to develop those skills yourself.

■ Questions

1. What type of education is most suitable for your goals?
2. Do you have a schedule for all the steps to be taken in the college admissions process?
3. How will you get the most from your college education?

■ ■ ■

Young Children's Education

Just as with colleges, there are public and private primary and secondary schools. Public schools are funded mainly by property taxes, whereas, private schools are supported by tuition fees and donations. Each state has school boards that set guidelines for their local district schools.

Primary schools include kindergarten (from age 5) and elementary school (usually from age 6). Secondary schools include junior high (grades 6 through 8) and high school (grades 9 through 12). This can vary by state. There are also schools for special needs, for example, for children with a physical or learning disability.

There are many exchange programs and international educational opportunities available for children and especially teenagers. I have not heard of anyone regret their experience. The Council on Standards for International Educational Travel (CSIET) prints an *Advisory List of International Educational Travel and Exchange Programs*. It lists over 60 international programs, with the countries of participation, costs, program specifics. You can get it for about $10 by calling ☎1-703-739-9050. Most of these programs are for students age 13 to 18.

Education is accessible to everyone. In public schools, you will find children from various religious, racial, and economic backgrounds. And they are often taught by as many various teachers.

■ The Influence of Teachers

"The future belongs to those who believe in the beauty of their dreams." — Eleanor Roosevelt.

As parents, you are not the only influence on your children. The importance and value of dedicated teachers cannot be stressed enough. The way a teacher behaves with a student can either make dreams soar or crash. Let me relate two examples from my own life.

I attended first grade in a small school in Lithuania. One day I went to school with laryngitis. The teacher asked me about my homework assignment in front of everybody. I pointed to my throat and whispered that I cannot speak. Rather than going to another student, the teacher persisted. She asked me to explain the assignment anyway. I tried. It sounded funny. The whole class laughed. I don't remember if the teacher laughed also, but I felt so embarrassed that I still remember the incident.

A quite different experience occurred in the tenth grade in Maryland. We were asked to write a short story about our earliest memories. I wrote about my country. When the papers were returned the following week, the teacher announced that she selected to read the best story to the whole class. It was my story. She read it with emphasis and emotion. I felt so proud. The applause from my classmates inspires me to this day.

Teachers have the power to effect the future of each student they teach. It is crucial that you, as a parent, be involved in your child's education. Get to know the teachers. How are they influencing your child? What are their expectations? What are the homework assignments? How is your child doing? How can you help?

■ Other Influences

"The thing that impresses me most about America is the way parents obey their children." — Edward, Duke of Windsor.

Other kids will probably have the most influence on your children. Your children will probably become "Americanized" very quickly. This often comes as a shock to newcomer parents. They are surprised how quickly their children learn English and how quickly they establish friendships. Like in all countries, there are good and bad friends.

One constant pressure on your children will be to conform to what other kids are doing, the parties they go to, how much or how little they study, etc. Most kids want to be "cool," a term used to describe someone who is popular, someone who has a lot of friends. Unfortunately, in most American children's eyes, foreigners are not "cool." This could cause your children a lot of stress. They may be tempted to do things to become more popular. Parents need to be aware of these pressures. And, of course, there are no easy answers on how to handle it.

There are bullies in every school, kids that tease, threaten, and beat up other kids. Your children may be perfect victims for this kind of abuse. If the teacher is not willing or able to handle situations that may come up, encourage your children to go to the principal of the school. Teach your children to use their sense of humor and imagination to solve problems, not their fists. If they use their fists, the bullies may choose a knife or a gun. It sounds incredible, but it happens every day.

Another influence on your children will be the media — mainly television and movies. Programs in America are often too violent and negative. And kids simply spend too much time watching them. Rather than playing outside with their friends, being creative, learning social skills, they sit in front of the TV. By most professional opinions, it is a good idea to limit what your children watch.

Drugs are a big problem in this country. By the time youngsters become seniors in high-school, 40% of them try drugs. Even one out of four eighth-graders try illegal drugs. It is important not to avoid this subject with your kids. They need to know what drugs can do to their bodies and brains. And they need these discussions often. If kids don't hear their parents views, they will only have their friends' views to act on. Studies show that the more parents talked about the dangers of drugs, the less likely were their children to try them.

Since most drugs are offered by friends from school, your child needs ways to respond without feeling he will lose all possible friendships. He could say that if he does drugs he won't be accepted on the basketball team, or that he knew someone that got really sick from it, or that Mom and Dad always wait up for him to get home and will catch him right away. Your child must be encouraged to find new friends, that don't experiment with drugs.

Children who are kept busy — homework, dance class, music lessons, athletics — are less likely to experiment with drugs. If they are busy with uplifting, challenging activities, they are less likely to look for drug-induced stimulation. The U.S. Department of Health and Human Services provides free information on drug abuse. Call ☎1-800-624-0100 to order two booklets called *Growing Up Drug Free: A Parent's Guide to Prevention* and *Preventing Drug Use Among Children and Adolescents*. The booklets discuss the facts about various drugs and what children need to know at different age levels.

■ **Questions**

1. In what ways are children different in this country?
2. Do you communicate often with your child's teacher?
3. Who influences your children the most?

■ ■ ■

If You Didn't Finish High School

Education plays a major role in the ongoing immigration debate. Highly-skilled immigrants, particularly those with advanced degrees, are being welcomed and unskilled, uneducated workers are not. Research shows that immigrants with a high school education or above are considered to be "net contributors" to society while those without a high school degree are "a burden" to taxpayers throughout their lifetime. Is that a stigma you wish to live with?

If you left high school without graduating, here or in your country, you can take a General Educational Development (GED) Test. A GED Diploma is an equivalent to a high school diploma and is accepted to get into most colleges and universities. The test is available throughout the entire U.S., in English, Spanish, and French.

Call the department of education in your state and ask for the testing center nearest to you. For GED publications, you can also call ☎1-301-604-9073 or write to:

GED Fulfillment Service
P.O. Box 261
Annapolis Junction, MD 20701

Practice tests are available by calling Steck Vaughn Co. at ☎1-800-531-5015.

▪ Question

1. If you don't have a high school degree, what steps will you take to pass the GED exam?

MONEY

Internal Revenue Service (IRS) — Taxes

The Internal Revenue Service (IRS) is the largest law-enforcement agency in the U.S. with over 110,000 employees and 600 offices. It exists to make sure that people pay their required taxes. It is very important for all citizens and residents of the U.S. to have a good understanding of current tax laws and have a general understanding of the huge agency that enforces them.

Compliance to IRS tax laws is based on the honor system. However, the honor system is greatly scrutinized. IRS auditors will come after you, if they suspect you didn't pay enough. First, understand that to <u>minimize or avoid</u> taxes by legal means is fine. To <u>evade</u> paying taxes by hiding or misrepresenting financial transactions is <u>not</u> fine. (Martin Kaplan, CPA, 1995.) So when you avoid paying taxes this year on any tax-deferred investments, it is legitimate. But when you inflate business expenses, it is not. There are multitudes of books on taxes but the laws are constantly changing. This section is meant to serve as a general guideline. You can get the most up-to-date information from a tax professional or directly from the IRS.

The system for tracking taxes goes like this. Upon starting a new job, your employer lets you fill out Form W-4 to show the number of exemptions you claim. If you are the head of the household, your spouse does not work, and you have two children, you could choose to claim four exemptions. Exemptions reduce the taxes withheld from your paycheck by your employer.

You can change your exemptions if you anticipate having a lot of deductions for any specific year. Deductions are the legal ways to minimize taxes. The year that we bought our house we had a lot of deductions. We increased our exemptions at the beginning of that year, and thus increased the size of each paycheck. The deductions at the end of the year balanced everything out. If your employer holds back too much taxes from your paycheck, you are lending the IRS your money and getting no interest on it. Even if a large refund at the end of the year appeals to you, it is not smart.

At the end of each year, every person above a certain income level must file income tax forms (often called a "return") with the state and federal government. These forms are available at any post office or library. Depending how much of your income went to pay taxes, you may receive a refund or you may owe more. You must file your taxes before April 15 or apply for an extension.

Depending on your income level, you may qualify for earned income credit (EIC), a refund of federal taxes withheld, plus other tax considerations. In 1997, a family earning less than $25,760 and raising one child may qualify, as well as a family earning less than $29,290 and raising two or more children, or a single worker with less than $9,770 in income. The income level requirements do change, however, so check it out. If you think you qualify, call the IRS at ☎1-800-829-3676 and order publication 596, *Earned Income Tax Credit*. Ask your employer about getting the credit with each paycheck, called <u>advanced earned income tax credit payments</u>.

Do not be a naïve taxpayer. If the IRS finds that you owe more money than you paid, getting the money from you comes before any legal rights you have as a U.S. resident or citizen. And they won't just ask for additional taxes. They will add on interest and penalties. You will also not be granted U.S. citizenship if you owe taxes.

The following true story is an example of what can happen to many newcomers. For privacy reasons, the names are not provided.

A young family moved to America. The young father was a respected physician in his country and accepted a fellowship offer at a research hospital. So much promise, such eagerness to learn, such willingness to contribute. He came to be a doctor, not thinking that the IRS first wants him as a taxpayer. After opening his own private practice, he hired an accountant that was highly recommended. For four years, the accountant kept track of the doctor's financial transactions and filed his annual tax returns. The doctor was left to take care of his patients. Seemed like a good arrangement. What did the IRS think of it? They demanded that the doctor pay a tax debt of $200,000.

Even if you hire an accountant to do your taxes, you must learn the basics yourself. This is the advice of many immigrants who learned the hard way. Trust your accountant, but understand the basics of the system so you can catch obvious errors. And always remember that an accountant is not an attorney. Whatever you tell an accountant could legally be revealed in the court of law.

For more information or any tax-related question, you can dial the IRS Tax Help line, ☎1-800-829-1040. The IRS also offers free tax services and over 100 useful, free publications. Call ☎1-800-829-3676 and ask for publication 910, *Guide to Free Tax Services*. You can choose which services and publications would be useful to you.

■ Questions

1. How can you legally minimize your taxes?
2. Do you understand the basic U.S. tax laws?

■   ■   ■

Paying Bills

 No matter how much money you make, it has a way of slipping through your fingers. Money goes to pay for rent, to pay for your car, food, education, medical treatment, for furniture, credit cards, and so many other things. These things are called bills.

If you came to America as a refugee, you may be receiving some federal assistance. Or your relatives may support you in the very beginning. You probably know that, no matter how wealthy your American relatives are and how much they are willing to help you now, they cannot help you forever. Financial independence is highly valued in America. It is a skill that needs to be learned and managed. It is how you can start to build a quality life for yourself.

As you start to gain financial independence, you will be incurring your own bills. The most important ones to pay on time, the ones that will start to build your credit worthiness are your rent, utility bill (water and electricity), telephone bill, and car loan, if you have one. For people with no other credit history, your bill payments will be reviewed should you decide to buy a home or apply for a loan in the future. Keep all payment receipts showing the date you made each payment.

Paying Yourself

Now that you have been told to always pay your important bills on time, please add paying yourself as one of those important bills. Whatever you need to buy, whomever you owe money to, take 10% of your monthly salary and save it. It is the only way to secure your financial future.

A systematic, regular investment program is the best way to grow the confidence and resources that will be necessary to fulfill your dreams in America. If you have the discipline to save money, you will have the discipline to accomplish a lot in America.

■ Questions

1. What are some bills you currently have?
2. How much can you "pay yourself" each month?

Banks and Credit Unions

Only after many years in this country, did I understand what exactly was a credit union. I kept reading and seeing on television about union strikes, membership dues for unions, union contracts, and other associations with the word "union." I thought a credit union was something like a labor union. As you learn English, you may have similar misunderstandings. Let us compare credit unions to banks.

A credit union is a financial institution that operates much like a bank, but is non-profit and provides more benefits for its members. Most banks charge fees for checking accounts, many even on savings accounts, fees on using automated teller machines (ATM's), sometimes even fees for using tellers (bank employees). A credit union provides the services of a bank, but usually with less fees. Banks often require that you maintain a minimum balance in your account (industry average is $300). Credit unions may require as little as $5 just to keep the account open. Also many credit unions pay interest on both, checking and savings accounts, and offer credit cards and loans at lower interest rates.

Whenever you have the opportunity, through an employer, school, association or a family member, join a credit union, even if it is in another state. I live in Maryland but joined a credit union in Pennsylvania. All my transactions are done by telephone or mail.

There are credit unions that are formed by various nationality groups. Each has its own set of guidelines for membership. There are credit unions for Ukrainians, Russians, Chinese, Taiwanese, Koreans, Lithuanians, Latvians, and many others. Perhaps there is one for your nationality's community.

To find a credit union that you may be able to join, contact the Credit Union National Association (CUNA), ☎1-800-356-9655, to get a phone number for the credit union representative for your state. The local representative is your best resource to credit unions in your area and qualification guidelines.

If you don't qualify for any credit union, you will need banking services. Visit a few banks near your home and check their fees and interest rates. Make sure the bank you choose has safety deposit boxes available. You will need to rent one for a small fee to keep important documents and valuables.

If you have your employer directly deposit your paychecks into your account, some banks will reduce checking fees. Ask about other ways that fees can be reduced. Open up a bank checking account so you can write checks, and put some money in a savings account for your basic monthly spending and emergencies. Then invest a portion of your money. You can start investing slowly as will be described in the next few sections. It is not recommended that you buy investments offered by banks, except an occasional certificate of deposit (CD) for short-term secure savings. Banks often charge high commissions for the investments they offer.

Banks may ask to see various documents in order to open an account. The usual documents requested are a social security card (which you can get from the Social Security Administration, ☎1-800-772-1213, for banking purposes, even if you don't have a green card to work), a driver's license, and possibly a school or employee identification card. If you are classified as a non-resident alien, you will need to file form W-8, *Certificate of Foreign Status*, which the bank should provide or you can get by calling the Internal Revenue Service (IRS), ☎1-800-829-3676.

Either way, bank or credit union, <u>your combined deposits are insured up to $100,000</u>. (That means if the bank goes bankrupt, you will get your money back, up to $100,000.) However, whether you choose a bank or a credit union, current savings interest rates have not kept pace with the inflation rate. Savings interest rates are very low and taxable. Inflation often eats up any growth. At 4% inflation rate, $100 today will be worth $67 in 10 years. If you are getting 2-3% interest, you are still behind. It costs you dearly, to keep all your money in the checking or savings account. You will need to find investments that return an average of 10-15% per year.

■ Questions

1. Is there a credit union you could join?
2. Why should you invest a portion of your money?

Financial Planners

There are many qualified financial consultants that could help you with your investment strategies. If your situation is very complicated and involves a lot of money, consulting a specialist is important. Choose one that is <u>fee-only</u>. This means that they get paid a flat rate by each client and have no incentive to sell you anything. A <u>commission-based</u> adviser earns a percentage of each transaction.

There are respected organizations that provide referrals to fee-only advisers. The Licensed Independent Network of CPA Financial Planners (LINC) can refer you to a fee-only planner that is also a licensed Certified Public Accountant (CPA), ☎1-800-737-2727. The National Association of Personal Financial Advisors (NAPFA) also refers to fee-only planners, ☎1-888-333-6659. Also, *Worth Magazine* publishes a "Top 200 Advisers List."

If your money situation is not complicated (but you just seem to never have enough of it), you can take control of your financial future by learning more about investing and starting on your own. With the strategy in the next section, you can start quickly by yourself. Don't wait until you know everything possible about stocks, bonds, portfolio diversification, etc. There are simple ways you can start to invest small amounts of money and learn as you go.

■ Questions

1. What are some investment terms you understand?
2. Do you need a financial planner?

How to Grow Your Money

When it comes to money, it is more important what you are able to keep, than what you actually make. What you <u>keep</u> is comprised of what money you set aside and <u>don't spend</u>, how much of it you can <u>grow</u>, and how much you are legally able to <u>shelter</u> from taxes. We will discuss all three.

Paying yourself <u>first</u> is a great way to catch a little of your money before it is gone. A good strategy is to take at least $50 from every monthly paycheck, before you spend it, and make it grow. But where will you put the monthly $50? If you go to a bookstore or library you will see walls full of books and magazines on the subject of money. They are often written using difficult investment language, describing all possibilities available with various opinions and speculations. It could get very confusing.

There are riskier investments and safer investments. We already know that putting money in a bank is safe but costly. Depending on bank fees and inflation, leaving your money in a bank could be no more profitable than putting it under your mattress.

So we know we should invest. But where? In <u>stock mutual funds</u>. There are thousands of mutual funds to choose from. First, what is a stock mutual fund? It is a pool of money from individual investors that is used to buy shares of various company stocks. Purchasing bits and pieces of many stocks automatically spreads the risk. The funds and all transactions are managed by investment professionals. There are also bond mutual funds that invest in various bonds, money market funds that invest in various securities, and other types of mutual funds. We will focus on <u>stock</u> mutual funds. Historically and long-term, they perform better than other mutual fund options.

This is the procedure for investing in stock mutual funds:

1) Call each of the mutual fund "families" listed below (or any others that you know something about). You may be prompted by a recorder or you may speak with a person. Say something like this — "I am interested in investing in no-load stock funds, especially in <u>inter-</u>

national, mid-cap (mid-size companies) and small-cap (small companies). Please send me a prospectus on what you have and an automatic monthly investment application." Some monthly minimums are listed below (confirm everything with the company representative):

- American Century – ☎1-800-345-2021. No minimum to start, $50 per month until you reach $2500.

- Harbor Funds – ☎1-800-422-1050. $500 minimum to start, $100 every 3 months or every month until you reach $2000.

- T. Rowe Price Funds – ☎1-800-638-5660. No minimum to start, $50 per month until you reach $1000.

- Neuberger & Berman – ☎1-800-877-9700. $100 minimum to start, $100 per month until you reach $1000.

These fund families have been around for many years, are well-recognized, do not require large initial deposits, have no up-front commissions, have performed well in the past with average annual returns of 10-15%, and are a good place to start. You can certainly choose from others as well. (If you read about a mutual fund company that sounds good, you can always get its phone number by dialing ☎1-800-555-1212 and ask for the toll-free number for the specific company.) If you are investing in an IRA (discussion to follow), minimums are usually only $250 to $500 for most mutual fund companies. In this case also get a prospectus on any available index funds (the Vanguard Index500 is especially attractive due to its low expenses). No mutual fund guarantees a specific rate of return. And no mutual fund is insured by the government. The growth depends on how the fund's stock choices perform.

2) When the mutual fund information arrives, look through each prospectus, check investment strategies, fund management expenses (industry average is 1.30% of assets), annual fees for small accounts (usually $10 per year for accounts with less than $2000). Choose one or two funds that you feel comfortable with, follow the directions to fill out the automatic investment application. Most investment companies will gladly do business regardless of your residency status. You

will have to mark whether you are a U.S. citizen, resident alien, or non-resident alien. Non-residents will most likely have to complete a W-8 form, *Certificate of Foreign Status,* to be exempt from U.S. taxes (the mutual fund company will send you one). The tax laws of your country of residency will apply. If you have questions about anything, keep calling the companies. <u>You are a potential client and they want to help you</u>. Mail the form and any initial deposit required.

3)   <u>You are in!</u> Money will be withdrawn on a specific day of each month according to how you requested, from your savings or checking account, and will be invested in the funds you specified. You will be paying yourself first. There is nothing more you have to do, except check on your funds periodically and declare them with your annual tax return. Millions of Americans are doing this. You will feel great that you did it!

Now you can take some time to learn about all the other excellent mutual funds available, the stock market, bonds, portfolio diversification, etc. Everything will make more sense, since you are now part of it. You can follow the progress of your funds in the business section of your local newspaper. Don't be alarmed by the ups and downs. <u>Historically and by many professional opinions, long-term investing in aggressive growth stock mutual funds is the best strategy</u>. You can take your money out at any time with no penalties, but don't do it when stocks are down.

So we know how to save a set amount per month and grow it for the future. So how do we shelter it from taxes so it grows even faster? We do this by growing it <u>tax-deferred</u> (not being taxed until you take the money out). One way is to ask these same fund companies mentioned above to set up your investment as a self-directed Individual Retirement Account (IRA). IRA money is meant for your retirement. You can withdraw from it at any time, but 20% will be automatically withheld for taxes and you may have to pay a 10% penalty if you withdraw before the age of 59½. The penalty may not apply if the withdrawal is due to disability, death, medical bills, a first home purchase, or for higher education expenses.

Whenever legally and financially possible, you want to put off paying taxes to a later date. Say you and I invest $2000 every year for 10 years and it grows 8% per year. The only difference is that you had the mutual fund company set it up as an IRA. At the end of 10 years, we each put in a total of $20,000 of our own money. In 30 years total, my account balance would read $160,000 and yours would read $244,000. You did much better. Upon retiring, you can take your money out, pay no penalty, and most likely pay less taxes.

Fully understand and take advantage of compounding interest and tax-deferment. Together, they are powerful. The money you invest earns interest, as well as the interest earns interest. The longer the money is left untouched and untaxed, the more dramatic the investment results will be.

■ Questions

1. What is a stock mutual fund and an IRA?
2. Do you have a long-term investment plan?

■ ■ ■

Retirement and Social Security

"You can be young without money but you can't be old without it." — Tennessee Williams.

In some countries, it is customary for children to take full financial responsibility for their aging parents. That may be difficult to expect in America. Each person must plan for his or her own retirement. The time to start saving for your retirement is when you are born. A $1000 investment made on the day you arrive home from the hospital would be worth over $1 million dollars when you turn 65. Of course, if you or your parents didn't start that early, the time to start is <u>now</u>. The younger you are, the less you will need to invest your own money, and the more compounding interest will do its magic, as we discussed earlier.

We will now discuss social security, what it is, what it does, and how it <u>supplements</u> your own retirement savings. Perhaps in other countries, retired people can more fully rely on social services for a comfortable future. Not so in America. The benefits paid will not be enough. According to the Social Security Board of Trustees, there are adequate resources to pay benefits in full for the next 34 years. If you are in your twenties, that may not sound very reassuring. With or without Social Security benefits, you will need more money.

The Social Security Administration (SSA) issues three types of social security cards: 1) the usual card listing the person's name and number, issued to U.S. citizens and permanent residents, 2) a temporary card that is not valid for work but can be used for identification, banking, etc., issued to foreigners, and 3) a temporary card that is valid for work, authorized by the Immigration and Naturalization Services (INS). The SSA tracks each individual's earnings so it can determine future retirement or disability benefits for the individual and any dependents. It is against the law to use someone else's social security card. To obtain a card of your own, call ☎1-800-772-1213 for more information and for the address of your local SSA office.

As you work for someone else or for yourself, part of your tax deductions go to pay into a social security fund. Besides paying federal, state and local taxes, 7.65% of each paycheck goes to grow social security. It is often listed as "FICA" taxes on your pay slip. Your employer also pays 7.65% for you. SSA splits the collected money into retirement, disability, and health insurance (called Medicare). If you are self-employed, you have to contribute both parts, a total of 15.3%. You must work and contribute into the system for a minimum of 40 quarters (10 years of work for most people) to be able to access social security benefits. A non-working spouse will receive 50% of what the working-spouse receives.

The normal retirement age, to receive full benefits, is age 65 if you were born before 1959. If you were born after 1959, your full retirement age is 67. Many people continue to work, at least part-time, as they collect their SSA money.

You do not want to be old, sick and poor in America. That is a terrible fate. So you need to look for ways to save more money for your retirement. The best long-term strategies for saving money for your retirement, according to many experts, are:

1) If you have a 401k plan through your employer (called 403b for government workers), maximize it to the fullest (often up to 16% of your salary is allowed, or a maximum total of about $10,000 per year). Cut your budget back a bit now, to have a lot more later. Your company benefits department has all the information you need to start and the investment options that are available. If you have more than five years left before you retire, direct at least 70% of your investments to aggressive growth, international funds, and common stock. The remaining 30% invest as you wish. Let time work for you. Don't touch this money prematurely. Pushing the 401k to the limit, before investing in any other tax-deferred plan, is a great idea because it reduces your taxable income. You reduce tax withdrawals from your paycheck and you put off paying taxes on your investment until you retire — a double bonus! On top of that, many employers match your contribution up to a certain percentage. For example, your employer may add another 50 cents for every dollar you put in up to 5% of your paycheck. Truly, one of the best ways to save for the future!

2) If you don't have a 401k or 403b option through work, another choice is the Individual Retirement Account (IRA), as we discussed before. Anyone that is earning income can contribute up to $2000 per year in a tax-deferred IRA. And a new tax law now allows another $2000 for a non-working spouse. If you have no other pension plan and are single and make less than $35,000 per year, or married and jointly make less than $50,000, you can also deduct your IRA contribution from your income, to pay less taxes. If you have more than 5 years left to retirement, invest your IRA money in stock mutual funds (the companies listed in the previous section are fine). If you have less than 5 years, and are nervous about the ups and downs of the stock market, put a portion of your IRA savings in certificate of deposits (CDs), money market funds, and other safer investments. <u>Note: Do not let any retirement money touch your hands until you retire. You will not only incur penalties and taxes, but you may also spend it.</u> Mutual fund companies can handle all transfer transactions from start to finish.

3) If you are self-employed, you have some good options for saving tax-deferred. IRAs are one option. The Keogh plan is another. Again you can set it up through a mutual fund company. Under this plan, you decide how much you want to contribute tax-deferred per year, up to $30,000. The Simplified Employee Pension Plan (SEP) is set

up similar to an IRA and allows tax-deductible contributions up to 15% of your compensation (or up to a maximum of $22,500). For all your options and current tax laws, call your mutual fund company or the Internal Revenue Service at ☎ 1-800-829-3676 and request publication 560, *Retirement Plans for the Self-Employed.*

Every three years you should get an estimate of your future social security benefits by calling SSA, ☎ 1-800-772-1213. You will be prompted by a recorder that will take down your name and address. If you speak with a representative, ask for a *Personal Earnings and Benefit Estimate Statement.* After you send in the completed form, you will receive a statement of how much you have been paying into the social security system and what your approximate future benefits will be. Also request SSA to send you the following booklets, as they pertain to you: *Social Security — Understanding the Benefits* (Publication 05-10024), *Retirement* (05-10035), *Survivors* (05-10084), and *Disability* (05-10029). Depending how close you are to the age of 65 or if you are disabled, you may also be interested in the booklet *Medicare* (05-10043), describing the basic health insurance program.

If you have reached retirement age, join the American Association of Retired Persons (AARP). Call them at ☎1-202-434-2277 for many free publications on housing, investments, legal advice, and retirement strategies. As a member of AARP, you are often entitled to many discounts at various establishments.

■ Questions

1. Do you have an investment plan for your retirement?
2. Does your company offer a 401k plan?

Building Your Credit History

One of the most valuable assets in America is a good credit history. If you consistently pay your bills on time, you are more likely to be granted additional credit, such as loans and credit cards.

There are three major credit reporting bureaus: Experian (☎1-800-682-7654), Equifax (☎1-800-685-1111), and Trans Union (☎1-800-916-8800). These companies compile data on people's credit worthiness and sell it to creditors who ask for the information. If you have a credit card or have taken out a loan for school, or to buy a car or a home, this information becomes part of your credit history. Financial institutions, stores, and employers can have access to your credit report.

If you think you have started accumulating credit information, you can obtain a copy of your report by calling the above telephone numbers. You will be instructed on how to get the report. Experian provides one free copy each year. Send your request in writing, showing your full name, your spouse's name, your addresses for the past five years, social security number, date of birth, and a copy of your driver's license or any bill statement verifying your current address. Sign the request and send it to Experian, Attn: NCAC, P.O. Box 949, Allen, Texas 75013-0949. They have brochures in English and Spanish to explain the credit reporting service. Any negative financial information will be reported for 7 years. Information about bankruptcies will be reported for 10 years.

Stay away from companies that advertise "instant credit, no matter what your previous credit history." They are often not reputable companies. To start building credit history, you need to obtain credit from a reputable company or bank that reports to the major credit bureaus. Try to obtain a charge card at your local department store. You may be able to get approved for a card with a small charge limit, such as $250.

If you can't find a store or bank that will issue you credit because you don't have any credit history, consider taking out a secured loan. For example, you can go to a bank, deposit $1000 in a savings account or CD (certificate of deposit), and take out a $1000 loan. Many banks will gladly give you a secured loan. The bank would freeze your $1000 until you pay back their $1000. Make your monthly payments <u>before the due date</u> over 12 to 24 months, depending what the bank offers. Call around for the lowest loan interest rate. Just make sure that your payment history will be reported to the major credit bureaus. And make sure your deposit earns interest and is completely safe, unless you fail to repay the loan. The same could be done with certain credit card companies, as will be discussed under the next heading.

If you don't have $1000 or so to put down for security, try to find someone, perhaps a relative, who will co-sign on your loan. This means that they will guarantee that you will pay the loan back. The bank will then check the credit history of your co-signer and decide whether to approve the loan. Again, check to make sure the bank will report to the credit bureaus.

Begin to build a good credit history as soon as possible. Whenever you are rejected for credit, find out why. Is it because of your credit history, your income, your length of time on the job, or something else? Call the credit bureaus and request a copy of your credit report. The report is free if requested within 30 days of the rejection letter.

■ Questions

1. Do you pay your bills on time?
2. What will you do to build a good credit history?

■ ■ ■

Credit Cards — a Blessing and a Curse

When it comes to purchasing things, if you could adopt the "if I can't afford it, I don't want it" mentality, you will be ahead of most people financially. Yes, you will get into debt when you purchase a home, perhaps when you purchase a car, and you will have other monthly obligations as was discussed earlier. But try not to get in trouble with credit cards.

Credit cards are very popular in America because Americans like to "buy now and pay later." There are many types of credit cards. Major credit cards are ones like Visa, MasterCard, American Express, and Discover for purchasing just about anything, anyplace. Store credit cards are ones like Sears, Montgomery Ward, and JC Penny's for purchasing store items. There are also service station credit cards like Exxon, Amoco, and Shell for purchasing gasoline and car repair services.

The most widely accepted credit cards are Visa and MasterCard. Some of the largest issuers are Citicorp, ☎1-800-462-4642, AT&T, ☎1-800-662-7759, Household, ☎1-800-477-6000, Chase Manhattan, ☎1-800-482-4273, and First USA, ☎1-800-537-6954. As a newcomer, you may have trouble getting a major credit card, due to your lack of credit history. If that is the case and you keep getting denied, you may have to apply for a "secured" credit card. This means you will make a deposit with the credit card issuer, to be held as collateral. Your deposit may be as low as $300 and will earn interest. It will be held in case you fail to pay what you owe on your credit card. If you close the account, you will get back your deposit, plus interest of about 3% to 5%. The following issuers offer secured credit cards: Chase Manhattan Bank, ☎1-800-482-4273, Orchard Bank, ☎1-800-688-6830, Citicorp, ☎1-800-743-1332, Federal Savings Bank, ☎1-800-285-9090, and Capitol One, ☎1-800-333-7116. Check their annual fee rates and interest rates paid on your deposit.

Often it is not only more convenient but safer to pay with a credit card. I once worked for a company that went bankrupt. The customers who paid their deposits by credit card got 100% of their money back. The ones that paid by check or cash were able to get back only 20% of what they paid.

Credit cards are good for establishing credit history, for making travel reservations, for purchasing products or services over the telephone, and as a convenience so you don't have to carry a lot of cash. However, if you view credit cards as "free money" you will get in deep trouble financially.

If you find yourself in trouble, with many debts, with creditors calling you to pay up, contact the Consumer Credit Counseling Service (CCCS) in your area. Look in the phone book for the nearest location. Don't wait for your accounts to be turned over to collection services. CCCS is a non-profit agency with over 850 locations in all 50 states. Its sole purpose is to help people manage their bill paying and money problems. The service is usually done for free. They won't make the bills go away, but they will set a budget that will help repay them on an acceptable basis to you and your creditors.

■ Questions

1. Have you applied for a major credit card?
2. What steps will you take to make sure you or your family members don't overspend?

MAJOR PURCHASES

Language Difficulties

 When it comes to making major purchases, good communication skills are irreplaceable. Don't worry if you don't speak English well. You can still communicate effectively. You are a customer. Anyone who wants your business will be patient. If they are not, go someplace else.

Whenever you are face-to-face with another individual, you can work out most communication difficulties using your hands, signs, dictionaries, other people's help. Even with limited English, you will usually get your point across. This is more difficult over the telephone. A frustrated American that cannot understand you may simply hang up the phone.

If you are planning an important meeting or making an important telephone call and you don't speak English well, you obviously want to get a bilingual relative or friend to help you. If you are in a situation where no bilingual help is available, you may want to use the AT&T Language Line service that provides interpretation in 140 languages. If you have a major credit card (Visa, MasterCard, American Express, Discover) you can use the service.

If you are in a buying situation, especially if you are making a major purchase and are having trouble communicating, the person or company you are buying from may choose to pay for the service. Real estate companies, mortgage lenders, automobile dealers may all volunteer to pay for the service to attract your business. You can be sitting in the same room, just talking on different telephone lines. Simply dial ☎1-800-528-5888. Have the language request, credit card, and the number you are calling ready. It is available 24 hours a day with no appointment and the cost ranges from $4.15 to $7.25 per minute, depending on the language selected. Call the same number for specific details and a free demonstration of how the process works.

■ Questions

1. How can you be prepared for the most effective communication?

2. Call the AT&T Language Line for a free recorded demonstration.

■ ■ ■

Basics of Negotiating

"Negotiation is the highest form of communication used by the lowest number of people."—President John F. Kennedy.

Humor break:
Dad: "I'll pay you 50 cents to wash my car this week. And if you do it next week I'll raise it to a dollar."
Son: "I'll start next week then."

The motto of successful people is: "You don't get what you deserve, you get what you negotiate." Negotiation is best defined as communication with a purpose for a win/win agreement. (Roger Fisher, 1981.) When the resulting agreement is win/lose, it is not considered to be successful negotiation. Everyone negotiates, even though they may not call it that. Businessmen negotiate, politicians negotiate, students negotiate, buyers negotiate, spouses negotiate, children negotiate.

Negotiation skills are highly valued in America. If you can develop these skills, you will save money, make better decisions, and have a lot more satisfaction. When it comes to purchasing something, keep in mind that most decisions are not about people, they are about <u>things</u>. You can become a successful negotiator by confronting the things or the problem, never the people. Always keep in mind that your relationships with the people you are negotiating with are valuable. You may need these people again. See yourself as a partner not an opponent.

When negotiating for anything have a plan in mind. Although you should start from a position of friendly trust, successful negotiating requires a little bit of skepticism. It is often hard to know if other people are using tricks. For example, some car salespeople go in the back to try "to help you get the best price" by talking to the manager. Often they hide for a few minutes and come back saying, "I did all I can, this is the best price possible." Or they may come back with a position of "take it or leave it." Don't be afraid and don't give in.

Learn to recognize when people are using tricks, ask them if they want to reach a fair agreement and negotiate in spite of their tricks. If you call someone a liar, he will only stick to his position to prove that he is not. If someone is hostile, ask for his advice to soften him up and look for an option that is good for both of you. Have other options in mind so that if everything fails, you can walk away.

When it comes to major purchases, the key goal is to buy the right thing, in the best quality available, for the best possible price. When I graduated from college, I got a job as a Buyer for a major corporation. They put me through an extensive training schedule, teaching me how to prepare requests for quotation, analyze proposals, and negotiate the best price. What they spent very little time on was <u>evaluating quality</u>. The focus was on immediate cost savings. I was in charge of purchasing temporary services and office supplies. I learned that cheap paper jams up copiers, that poorly-paid temporary workers don't come to work, that the lowest-priced supply companies are often out of stock. Our "cost savings" cost us a lot of money. There is a famous saying: "You get what you pay for." Don't go for the cheapest. Go for the best quality you can afford to buy.

By knowing what you plan to buy, doing the research to know what is the best quality available, and matching it with what you can afford (or waiting until you can afford it), your next move is to negotiate your best price. <u>Always ask for the lowest price of the best quality item</u>. So many people forget to do that. They think if the price tag on the mattress is $500, then it must be $500. No. You may be able to get it for $465. You will never know unless you ask.

If you are over the age of 60, there are many senior citizen discounts available. Ask for it. If you are a student, there are discounts for you as well. Ask for them. If you are a consultant, for example, a home decorator, most retail shops that sell lamps, carpets, fabrics, etc., will gladly give you a discount, if you show them your business card. Whatever your situation, why not ask for a discount?

When negotiating for a lower price or better service, the key thing to remember is to never accept a "no" answer from someone who could not give you a "yes" from the very beginning. Talk to the <u>right person</u>. Learn how to be assertive, not aggressive. Be confident, not arrogant. It's alright to complain when service has been poor or the price is too high. Confidently ask for more, expecting the right person to deliver what you want.

■ Questions

1. How have you negotiated in the past?
2. What do you need to buy soon and how will you negotiate for it?

■ ■ ■

Buying a Car

It is very difficult to live in America without your own car. Public transportation is limited. You will eventually need to buy a car. First you will need to obtain a driver's license, if you don't have one yet.

You can get a driver's guidebook for free at all offices of the Motor Vehicles Administration (MVA, or also known as the Department of Motor Vehicles - DMV). Call ☎1-800-555-1212 and ask for the "800 number for Motor Vehicle's Administration Information" for your state. Call the 800 number and ask for the nearest location where to get the driver's guidebook, what exactly you need to do to get your license, and whether the law test is available in your language. Get the guidebook and learn the rules of the road. When you feel ready to take the test, go to the MVA. Bring your passport, your driver's license from your country, if you have one, and any other identification you have (such as a social security card or any other documentation proving your signature). You can get a driver's license even on a tourist visa.

To get your license, you may need to attend a 3-hour drug and alcohol class, pass a vision test, law test and a driving test. It will cost about $40. The law test is available in many languages, not just English. In Maryland, for example, it is available in Korean, Spanish, Russian, and Polish. Also translators are available to handle questions in many languages. But, whenever you go to the MVA, whether for your license, to register your car, or for any service, bring a friend or family member with you. Don't be surprised if they are just as lost as you are. Of course, your friend will not be able to act as your translator for any of the tests. Those you must do yourself. It is common to fail the law test on the first try. Don't despair if you do. Try again. You will eventually pass.

Okay. You got your license, you saved some money and now you are ready to buy a car. Unless you know exactly what you want to buy and have plenty of money, the smartest thing to do is to start your search not by going to display lots featuring shiny, new cars, but by going to the library. Go to the magazine section and find the publication *Consumer Reports*. Find issues that discuss and evaluate new and used cars. The April issue evaluates a lot of cars.

New cars lose about 20% of their value in the first year, so your better value will be a good used car. *Consumer Reports* lists price ranges, evaluates maintenance records, and makes recommendations for best buys. If you decide to buy or lease a new car, a lot of the paperwork will be taken care of by the dealer. That service is built into the price of the car. If you decide to buy a used car, you will need to handle more things yourself.

Let us say that you decide to buy a used car. While at the library, go to the information desk and ask to see the "blue book" on cars. This booklet officially prices all available cars by manufacturer and year. It lists available options and shows the trade-in value, bank loan value, and retail value. (Ask the librarian to show you all the numbers.) Keep in mind that four-door small and mid-size cars will probably be less expensive and certainly demand lower auto insurance rates than high-performance sports models.

When you have decided on a few good options, start going to dealers or calling owners that advertise in the *Classified* section of the newspaper. You know what you are looking for and what you are likely to pay. When you find the cars you are looking for, test them out on the road and thoroughly inspect them. When you choose a car you like, ask if you can drive it to a mechanic for a full inspection. If you take it to an approved service station that does state inspections, and the car passes the requirements, you will obtain a certificate which you will need anyway to register the car. It will cost about $50 for a state inspection. Many people do this step after buying the car and find surprises. Get the car inspected <u>before</u> buying it. Any problems the mechanic finds could be used to negotiate the price of the car. Call the U.S. Department of Transportation Auto Safety Hotline, ☎1-800-424-9393, and they will tell you whether the car has ever been recalled (asked to be returned for repairs) by the manufacturer. Have the repairs been done?

An often overlooked source of cars is an auction. Auctions are held on specific days and are advertised in the local newspaper. Most have pamphlets they could send you, with their different rules and procedures. Buying at auctions could be the least expensive but also the most risky method. Cars are often sold "as is," meaning "take them with all their problems." If you know a lot about cars and have very little money to spend, you may be willing to investigate how to buy at an auction.

Let us assume that you found the right car, inspected it, negotiated the price using what you learned from your research at the library, and paid cash for it or were able to get a loan to buy it. Now what do you do? You have to move some papers around. Back to the MVA! If you bought from a dealer, they will help with some of the paperwork. Either way, here are the papers you will usually need to get the car registered in your name and on the road:

1) Insurance binder – Shop around for your best insurance policy (see **Insurance**). When you decide on the insurance company, they will send you an insurance binder (a document proving your car is insured).

2) State inspection certificate – If you bought a used car and it has not been inspected yet, you will need to do it. It will cost about $50 (more in some states) and take a couple of hours. If they find something wrong with the car, it will need to be fixed before they give you the inspection certificate. The inspection certificate is usually good for 3 months. You should be able to register your car within that time.

3) Original Title – This is a document you have to obtain from the seller of the car, proving ownership. Copies are not acceptable.

4) Federal odometer reading statement – This shows the mileage at the time the car transfers from one owner to another. It is usually found on the back of the title document.

5) Original bill of sale – This paper shows the price you paid for the car, signed by the seller. It will be used to determine the sales tax. For example, say you bought a car for $3500 from a woman in Maryland. The woman would have to write a statement that she sold you the car for that amount. You may also get a blank bill of sale form from the MVA. (It may have to be notarized. Most banks provide notary service.) The MVA will ask you to pay 5% sales tax, which is $175. You would also have to pay about another $100 to cover fees for title, tags and registration.

Always call the local full-service MVA office to check what

documentation is required, because requirements vary by state and they do change. As you prepare for your trip to the MVA, you would need to bring all of the required documents and your checkbook or cash in order to complete the registration of your car. When you first arrive to the MVA, go to the information area. There is usually someone there that could direct you to stand in the right line. Don't fill out any forms until you know what to fill out. If you bought the car using loan money from a bank, you will need the bank's address. The bank becomes a "lien holder" of the title. This means that you don't own the car until you pay the bank in full.

One final note about purchasing a car with a loan. Many people do this and it is very acceptable. Keep in mind that this is one bill you do not want to postpone or pay late. Not only will it hurt your credit history, but some banks will repossess (take back) the car if they don't get a payment within 30 days after the due date. They don't even have to give you a warning.

■ Questions

1. What type of car do you want to buy?
2. What do you need to do to get it legally on the road?

■ ■ ■

Buying Insurance

 Buying insurance can be a very confusing experience. According to the National Insurance Consumer Helpline (NICH), 90% of Americans purchase the wrong types of insurance or have the wrong coverage. Many people find out years later that they have been paying for policies that provide either too much or too little coverage. Call the NICH, ☎1-800-942-4242, and ask for the local phone number of your State Insurance Department. The State Insurance Department can

send you a publication showing typical prices charged by different insurance companies for home and auto insurance. This comparison will be useful when you are getting quotes.

There is an insurance policy available for almost anything. The six main insurance coverages you need to know about are described below: automobile, renter's, home, health, disability, life. This discussion is very brief. As you shop around for insurance, understand what is included in each policy and what is not included. Read everything carefully. Ask your family and friends what insurance companies they use. To get discounts take out combination policies, such as automobile and renter's, with the same company.

■ Automobile Insurance

Automobile insurance is required if you own a car. It protects your car and the other driver's car in the event of an accident. Again, call your State Insurance Department for a publication that shows typical prices charged by different insurance companies. Call a few of the companies to get a quote for your car. You will need to give them the year, make, model, and identification number of the car. They will want to know how many miles you plan to drive per year, your age, your employer, where you live, previous accident history.

The closer you live to a city, the more expensive your insurance premiums will be, due to the possibility of more accidents, vandalism, and crime. As you call around for quotes, everything you say is put in the computer. Don't change the information later, for example, the number of miles you plan to drive or previous accident history. This may cause suspicion and a higher rate may be quoted. Policy prices can range from $700 to a few thousand dollars per year. The insurance does not have to be paid all at once. It can be paid in installments throughout the year. Discounts are often available for anti-theft devices, good driving record, good grades for students, if you are married, if your car is not a sports model, if the car has an airbag, and many other discounts. Always ask.

The largest companies often provide the best rates. Call GEICO, ☎ 1-800-841-3000, to get two quotes: the <u>minimum</u> insurance required by law and the <u>recommended</u> insurance. Other large companies are Aetna, Allstate, and State Farm. Look in the telephone directory yellow pages under *Insurance* to find their local agents. You may be placed in a "high-risk" category for your first few years in this country. Your rates will be higher. Ask when you can anticipate a rate decrease if a good driving record can be maintained. As always, if you have trouble communicating in English, have a bilingual friend help you. In many cases, insurance can be initiated the same day over the phone.

Whatever policy you choose, it will come with a deductible, a minimum you will have to pay out of pocket for each claim. For example, if your deductible is $250 and you bump another car causing $450 in damage, you will pay $250, and your insurance will pay $200. The lower the deductible, the more you will pay to be insured.

If you borrow your friend's car, the car is still insured. However, if you get into an accident and it is your fault, the insurance company may state that you are not to drive that car anymore, or any future claims due to your fault again may not be covered.

■ Renter's Insurance

Renter's insurance is strongly recommended for all renters to replace belongings in the event of a robbery, fire or another incident. It may cost about $100 per year. Homeowner's and renter's insurance policies protect your belongings even outside of your home. I recouped almost the whole cost of my policy with one claim, when my car was vandalized and my briefcase was stolen. Renter's insurance is cheap and well worth it. You usually have to pay extra to protect expensive jewels, furs, computer equipment, and other items. It is always a good idea to videotape or photograph all your belongings and keep the records in a safety deposit box at your bank.

■ Home Insurance

Home insurance works basically the same way as renter's insurance. It is required for all homeowners. It protects you and the mortgage lender in the event your home is destroyed by fire or another catastrophe. You should get a policy that gives you replacement-cost coverage. For a $100,000 home, it may cost about $200 per year. You can usually get a discount if you combine your home (or renter's) insurance together with your automobile insurance.

▪ Health Insurance

Unlike in many countries, the U.S. does not have a national health plan that covers all citizens. Health insurance is crucial. Any sudden, serious illness within the family can wipe you out financially. If your employer does not provide health insurance, you will need to purchase a policy on your own. Depending on your health status, consider buying a policy with a high deductible (the amount you have to pay each year before the insurance becomes effective). This way you will at least be covered for major medical costs and your monthly premiums will be lower. For example, a $100 deductible for a family plan may require payments of $375 per month, whereas a $5000 deductible, would cost only $130 per month. You may also be able to get a high deductible for yourself and a lower one for your children. Blue Cross/Blue Shield is one insurance provider that offers different plans for different family members. Understand that without some type of health insurance, you may have to pay for services in advance or you may be turned away.

▪ Disability Insurance

Disability insurance is strongly recommended to generate some income in the event you become disabled and unable to work. Your chances of becoming disabled are far greater than your chances of dying prematurely. Get a disability policy that will pay benefits until you are able to perform in your specific occupation. The cost of it will depend on your age, the type of work you do, whether you smoke, and other factors. Social Security may also pay benefits, if you become severely disabled.

▪ Life Insurance

Life insurance is highly recommended if you are the main provider for your family. If your spouse also has a good income, you can postpone life insurance to save money. Life insurance pays your family in the event of your death. It should probably be called "death" insurance and not life insurance.

Purchase what is called a <u>term policy</u>, not a whole-life policy. For a $100,000 policy, you can expect to pay anywhere from $130 to $700 per year, depending on your age, whether you smoke, etc. If you are the sole provider for the family and you die, you want your family to receive at least 5 times your annual income. With anything less, and no other regular income, it will be difficult for your family to financially survive the tragedy. Two recommended companies that sell insurance over the telephone are USAA Life, ☎1-800-531-8000, and Ameritas, ☎1-800-552-3553. Before buying and signing anything, check your insurance company's current ratings record by calling Standard & Poor (S&P), ☎1-212-208-1527, or Moody, ☎1-212-553-0377. Look for a rating of "A". Avoid those below a "B". There are organizations that could help answer a lot of questions, for example, the American Council of Life Insurance, ☎1-202-624-2000. Call InsuranceQuote, ☎1-800-972-1104, and SelectQuote, ☎1-800-343-1985, for free information on low-cost term life insurance.

Buying insurance can really add up to a lot of money. Get the facts and buy what is required. As your financial situation improves, buy what you can to protect yourself and your family.

■ Questions

1. What type of insurance do you need now?
2. What research do you plan to do to get the right insurance at a fair price?

■ ■ ■

Buying a Computer

In America, computers are being sold at a faster rate than television sets. In the section on **Education**, we discussed the value of having computer knowledge and access to the Internet. If you don't already have a computer, you will most likely buy one in the near future. So it is no longer a question of whether to buy a computer or not. It is a question of what type of computer to eventually buy.

Computer technology is changing fast, but the minimum you should consider for most personal uses, for a small business, and to access the Internet are: 100 megahertz Pentium processor or higher, 16 MB of RAM, 1000 MB hard drive, CD-ROM drive, 1 MB video memory, sound card, VGA monitor, mouse, 28.8 modem speed or higher, loaded with Windows and a few other software packages. You can buy this type of system with an inkjet printer for under $2000. Check with *Consumer Reports* in the library for computer and printer ratings.

Many computer stores provide financing. You may have to show that you have a major credit card. Stores often advertise their discounts and financing options in the newspaper. Whatever they offer, you may be able to negotiate a lower price, free disks, or some free software. Some computer salespeople work on commission.

If you understand the basics of computers and know exactly what you want to buy, you can save a lot of money by buying a used computer. For the same system described above minus the printer, you may have to pay only about $800. One popular used computer provider is the American Computer Exchange in Atlanta, GA, ☎1-800-786-0717. You may have to pay about $40 for shipping, set up the system yourself when it arrives, and accept the fact that you will have no warranty service.

■ Questions

1. What are some retail and discount computer stores in your area?
2. Do you have a friend that can help you with the shopping and computer setup?

■ ■ ■

Owning a Piece of America – a Home

Just because you are very new to America, <u>do not skip this section</u>! You may be thinking that buying a home is completely out of your reach now. However, you need to start preparing early. There are some things you can do <u>now</u> to prepare to buy a home later. You will be way ahead if you understand the process now.

When my family first came over in 1972, we rented apartments, sometimes even furnished ones. We wanted to stay light, we moved where my parents could find work, and we did not want to be tied down to a lot of furniture or to a specific location. This may be a good strategy for any newcomer for the first few years.

But once you become a permanent resident of the U.S. and find the right job and the right location, you will most likely want to purchase a home. Homeownership is viewed as personal and financial success by many Americans. It provides a sense of belonging and security. By buying a home, you will get tax benefits, you will be investing your money, and you will get the satisfaction of owning a piece of America. So, where do you begin? Again, you need information.

■ Information is Freely Available

Besides your usual visit to the local library, there are organizations that are interested in helping you. One such organization is the Fannie Mae Foundation. Among other activities, the Foundation reaches out to immigrants with information on homeownership and would like to help first-time buyers like you. You can call the Fannie Mae Foundation at ☎1-800-688-4663. Tell them that you are a first-time home buyer and ask them to send you the free booklet, *Opening the Door to a Home of Your Own.* (It is available in English, Spanish, Korean, Chinese, Vietnamese, Russian, Polish, Portuguese, and Haitian Creole.) The Foundation will send you a guide plus a list of local lenders and housing counselors that can help you get started. For Spanish-speaking counselors call ☎1-800-782-2729. For a guide on how to become a U.S. citizen and how to become a homeowner you can request *The New Americans Guide* by calling ☎1-800-544-9213 for the English version and ☎1-800-693-7557 for the Spanish version (*Guia Para Nuevos Americanos*). The Fannie Mae Foundation may also contact the AT&T Language Line for interpreter services for other languages (see section **Language Difficulties.**)

■ The Process of Buying a Home

In brief, let us discuss the procedure of buying a home. When you buy a home, it is considered a purchase of <u>real estate</u>. You will hear this term often. There are real estate companies that employ real estate agents to help you find a home that suits you and one that you can afford. They typically sell existing homes or resale homes. If you are interested in a newly constructed home, you can talk directly with a representative of the builder. You should be able to get a *New Homes Guide* at your local supermarket. Also, most builders advertise their communities in local newspapers, usually in the weekend edition.

As a first-time home buyer, you will certainly need the help of a knowledgeable real estate agent or the builder's sales representative. Real estate agents must have a license, whereas, new construction sales representatives often do not, because they only represent their employer's property. Both types usually work on commission — they don't make money until they sell a home. Keep in mind, that although you ask an agent or a representative to help you, their first boss is always the <u>seller</u>. The seller's interests come first because the seller pays the commission. Let us discuss the usual process of buying a home.

Let's say that you decide to buy a home within 30 miles of the major city, in a nice neighborhood, with good schools. You go to a real estate agency and speak with an agent about what type of home you are looking for, what location, how many bedrooms, how many bathrooms, on how much land, what price range, etc. The real estate agent runs a computer listing of the homes that are available with those specifications, in your desired location, for your specific price range.

The real estate agent would probably "pre-qualify" you before running around showing you all your options. To pre-qualify means to ask you some questions about how much money you earn, how long you have been at your job, what your debts are, how much cash you have available to put down as a "down-payment" on a loan (initial cash required may be as low as 2% of the total price). You may also want to be pre-qualified by a mortgage lender, so you know what you can afford to buy.

You may not like all the personal questions you will get from agents and lenders, but by the time you settle on a specific home, actually close the deal, your whole financial history will have to be revealed. It's not just <u>you</u> because you are a foreigner. They have to do this with <u>everyone</u> who is not paying cash for the full price of the house. Buying a home is probably the single, most-expensive purchase anyone makes. If someone were to ask you for a large loan, wouldn't you also want to know everything?

After your pre-qualification, the real estate agent will most likely schedule some specific days to take you around to the homes for sale that match your requirements. This is when you especially want to be aware that the agent works for the seller, the person whose house they are showing you. If you fall in love with a particular house and act like you must have it, there is not much that you will negotiate off the price. It is best to always stay objective, to look for flaws you can use to negotiate, and act like you can always walk away from the deal.

When looking at various homes, always confirm with the agent what will stay and what will go. For example, the washer and dryer may go, but the swing set outside may stay. Know exactly what the price includes. Also talk with the seller if possible. Why are they selling? Is the neighborhood getting worse? Are there problems with the house? Don't be afraid to ask questions.

With new home construction, you sometimes cannot negotiate the selling price, but you may ask them to "throw in" upgraded carpeting, a free doorbell, an extra window, or something else that appeals to you. It doesn't hurt to ask. With resale homes, the seller's asking price is usually flexible. It pays to negotiate.

Let's say you find a resale home you like. You will <u>not</u> say to the agent, "this is the one we will buy." You could make an offer of a price <u>lower</u> than the asking price and <u>contingent</u> upon a satisfactory professional inspection. It is highly recommended that you invest the $200 or so to get the home inspected before buying it, especially if the home is older. You may also make your offer contingent upon some other benefits, for example, that the seller fixes the leaky faucet or leaves the washer and dryer. The real estate agent will then write everything out and take your offer to the seller, and usually tell you the next day whether the offer has been accepted or rejected. If your offer is unreasonable, it will surely be rejected. So be reasonable if you want the house.

■ Shopping for a Mortgage Loan

The seller accepts your offer! Is the house yours? Not yet. Now you need to be officially approved for a mortgage loan. This is a loan that usually has to be paid back on a monthly basis over 15 or 30 years. Home builders, banks, credit unions, mortgage lenders, and government agencies all have various financing programs, especially for first-time home buyers. Shop around. Lenders want your business.

One mortgage option to consider is the Federal Housing Administration insured loan, usually called an "FHA loan." This loan is usually easier to qualify for, requires only 2¼% down-payment and may offer assistance with closing costs. It is often used for first-time home buyers for loans of less than $151,725 (this figure may vary). FHA allows 29% of your gross monthly income to go to housing expenses and 41% of your income to go to total long-term debts. So if your family's combined income is $2500 per month, you should qualify for a mortgage of $725 per month, with another $300 allowed for other debts (such as student loans, credit cards or car loan).

Another possible choice for low and moderate income home buyers is Fannie Mae's Community Home Buyer's Program (CHBP). It requires lower down payments, lower closing costs that could be borrowed, and credit histories are obtained from other sources, not just credit bureaus. So, say your dream house costs $125,000. You will pay about $3000 for a down-payment, plus another $2500-$5000 in closing costs. If the interest rate on the loan is 7.5%, your payments with mortgage insurance would be approximately $900 per month for 30 years.

You will need to show sufficient income to be able to afford the home you plan to buy. By shopping around for the right mortgage you may be able to get lower interest rates and a less costly arrangement. Lenders advertise in the newspaper and you can use the listing that Fannie Mae sends you. As a smart buyer, you will most likely buy a home "below your means," meaning spending somewhat less than what you can afford, so you don't live paycheck to paycheck.

If you are very new to this country, you may have very limited or no credit history. The mortgage lenders will have to create one for you. They will create it by checking how you have been paying your rent, your telephone bill, your electricity bill, and any other loans you may have. This is why it is important that you pay your bills on time and keep your receipts. Lenders may also ask for references from employers, family, or friends. They will want to see what type of credit risk you are.

Once your mortgage loan is approved, a date will be set for the settlement meeting, the final transfer of title and money. Long before that date, you will be told what you need to do. Buying a home is a highly regulated business in the U.S. There will be a lot of papers. You will need homeowner's insurance. You will hear words like property tax, points, mortgage insurance, title insurance, escrow, homeowner's association fees. All these are normal and will be explained to you. Of course, you will be prepared with your own research and ask many questions.

The process of buying a home is often complicated. It involves careful research and smart decision-making on your part. However, owning a home, <u>in the right location</u>, will be one of the most satisfying experiences you will have in America. Plan for it now and do it right.

■ Questions

1. What will you do now to build your credit history and to improve your chances of qualifying for a mortgage in the future?
2. Have you ordered the free booklets available from the Fannie Mae Foundation?

PREPARING FOR THE RIGHT CAREER

A Third of Your Life

"Be not simply good; be good for something."
— Henry David Thoreau.

Most people spend more time planning a vacation than planning their entire life. For example, let us take a look at a newcomer's typical first visit to America. Before the person comes over, he will talk with his relatives, he will save his money, he will choose what he would like to see, get all his documents in order, read guidebooks, and carefully pack making sure not to forget anything. He will invest a lot of time and energy in preparation. But do most people do that with life, in general? Unfortunately, no.

A third of a person's life will be spent doing some type of work. Doesn't it make sense that each person put a lot of thought in what it is he or she wants to do? Work can be paid or unpaid, in the home or outside the home. For the most satisfaction in life, a person should be more excited about <u>being involved in doing the work</u> than any title that it may provide. A person who cannot find this type of satisfaction with work will often be bored and frustrated, watch the clock every day, wait for the weekends.

Four out of five people in the U.S. do not like their jobs. (William Bridges, 1994.) There could be many reasons for this. Some are afraid to make a change to a more suitable job. Some don't want to get the education required for new work. Some feel too trapped by their financial obligations to switch to a lower-paying but more enjoyable job. Some may enjoy certain people or some benefits in their current job that keeps them from looking elsewhere.

To test whether a job is right for you, ask yourself whether you are happy with what you do 80% of the time. There will always be some work requirements that you do not enjoy, but if you like what you do most of the time, you will succeed in your work. People who stay at jobs that do not use their skills, will eventually become miserable. They will be miserable for 8 hours every day. They will be miserable for another hour or longer that will most likely be spent in traffic. Subtracting another 8 hours that will be spent sleeping, how much is left for truly satisfying living? Devote your energies to seeking satisfying work that makes use of your skills and talents.

It is understandable that when you are very new to America, you may have to settle for any type of work that is available, just to survive. That is, hopefully, just a <u>temporary situation</u>. Your goal should be set for your next job and the next, until you find work that is satisfying and meaningful for you. Why? Again — quality of life. The very reason you came to America.

One immigrant summed it up this way: "Telling your grandchildren that your biggest accomplishment in life was coming to America will probably not impress them. They will ask — and then what did you do?"

In this section, we will explore the steps to choosing work that is right for us, work that will give each of us the most satisfaction. This is a three step process: 1) reflecting on the basic areas of life, 2) identifying a dream that suits our skills and personality, 3) assigning goals or action steps that progressively move us to fulfill that dream.

■ **Questions**

1. Is it important for you to enjoy your work?
2. Do you have a job now that uses your skills and talents?

■ ■ ■

What is Your Purpose?

A person who has no idea about his purpose becomes like a tourist who keeps stepping off at the wrong train stations. He arrives someplace, but it's never the right place. Your purpose is your life's control center. Your purpose may be obvious to you. If it is not obvious, you need to do some thinking and analysis.

When considering what your purpose might be, first think about all four basic life areas: family, profession, public service and religion. (Peter McWilliams, 1991.) Most people's lives can fit in these four general areas. You may spend some time in every area, but when considering your purpose, your life's navigator, it helps to narrow your focus to only <u>one</u> life area. How do you know which area is the best for you? The one that inspires you the most, the one that you think about the most, is your life area.

Once you have selected your life area, you are in a position to find your true purpose. Be careful that you are not misled by the wrong intentions. Be aware of your own hidden agendas. If, for example, you are intrigued most by the family area and you decide your purpose is to get married and raise three healthy, happy children, that's fine. But if your hidden agenda is to find a rich husband so you don't have to work, so you can impress your friends, you will most certainly experience problems.

You will only find your true purpose with good, noble, honest intentions. Here are only a few examples: to entertain others, to teach others, to improve your town, to serve God, to heal people in pain, to make a better product or service, to raise children, to keep your community safe. Many people decide that their purpose is "to help others." That is too general. Notice that all of the above examples can help others. <u>A more narrow, more specific purpose will be a better control center for your life</u>.

Are you wondering if simply having fun and enjoying yourself makes a good purpose? Well, think about it. Having fun provides only short-term satisfaction. Eventually you either become bored or tired of relaxing, drinking with friends, playing cards, or watching movies. Relaxation is important and is a great reward for hard work, but it makes a weak purpose for life. A good test whether you have a strong purpose, is to ask the question, "does it make a difference?"

When you have found your life's purpose keep it to yourself. Don't talk about it. It is sacred. Keep the roots deep within you. It is your compass for life. If you have selected the right purpose, it is rare that you will change it. You may change what dreams you follow, but your purpose will not change. For example, if you feel your purpose is to "heal people in pain," your dream may vary from becoming a physician, to a physical therapist, to a nurse, or to any other healing profession. <u>It may take a few tries before you find the right dream</u>. Your purpose is not so variable. It is the center that your potential dreams revolve around.

■ Questions

1. What life area – family, profession, public service or religion – holds most interest for you, that you think about the most?

2. What do you think is your purpose? (Do not share this with just anyone.)

■ ■ ■

What Dream Will Fulfill Your Purpose?

"When love and skill work together, expect a masterpiece." — John Ruskin.

Hopefully, you now know your life's purpose. The rest of this section will be much more meaningful if you do. A "dream" is your logical next step.

The following section describes how to go about choosing your dream, sorting your values, living a typical day in your dream job, committing to the dream you choose, and keeping quiet about your dream.

■ What if I Don't Have a Dream?

"Some people die at twenty-five and aren't buried until they are seventy-five." — Benjamin Franklin.

I can't say it any better. Everyone has a dream. Coming to America may have fulfilled one of your dreams. What now?

■ How to Choose a Dream

In order to choose your dream, you need to look inside your heart. Usually, what you love to do is what you are gifted at doing. (Marsha Sinetar, 1987.) You don't have to be the best in it. But it should feel right for you. A dream for your life is like a shoe for your foot. It first needs to fit. And the more you wear it, the more comfortable it will get.

When selecting your dream, one way to focus your thinking is to ask yourself a few questions: What would I do if I had a 100 percent chance of success? What is my ideal lifestyle? What did I really love to do when I was a child? What would I do if I only had one year to live? What would I do with the rest of my life if I won a million dollars? (If your answer to this is "go back to my country," the question applies the same. What would be your dream there?)

Think about the most satisfying experiences you have had in your life so far. Some of your happiest accomplishments may come from your childhood experiences, others from hobbies, others from doing volunteer work, others from work you are doing now. Write down what you remember about your best experiences. Analyze them. Are you happiest working with people, working with things, or working with data? Do you prefer to work with your hands? Do you prefer inventive thinking and using numbers and details? Do you prefer using your creative and artistic skills? No matter how ordinary your talents may seem to you, you will have a desire to use them. Your most challenging and happiest moments in your life come from using those talents.

A common mistake some people make is to choose a profession that "looks good" or "pays well." A woman who really enjoys cooking, creating recipes, and serving people may have a dream of working in a restaurant, and maybe even owning one. At the same time she may feel that catering to people could be viewed as servitude and that becoming a dentist would "look better" to her parents and society. If she squelches her dream in order to honor the opinions of other people, she will probably become not only a bad dentist, but yet another unhappy person.

When you have selected a few potential dreams that respond to your purpose, write them down on a piece of paper. Next to each one write down your capabilities and limitations. For example, your dream may be to start a child daycare center in your home. Your capabilities may be good skills with children, knowledge of early human development, and certification in emergency procedures. Your limitations may be that you already have two children of your own, there are no nearby playground facilities, and you have no license. After doing this for each dream, close your eyes and imagine what your next five years would be like if you tried each one. Look at the good and the bad. Choose the dream that gives you the most satisfaction.

One warning about dreams: money, fame or power, chosen as dreams to follow in life, are the wrong intentions. They will fail you miserably. They will send you in the wrong direction.

■ Sorting Your Values

"This above all: to thine own self be true." —William Shakespeare.

When choosing your dream, it helps to line up and prioritize your values. Values are strong, cherished beliefs. They become obvious through close self-examination. Be aware whether they are truly your values, and not someone else's.

Take a piece of paper and across the top write three headings: I always value, I sometimes value, I never value. Now underneath each heading, write the following values under the right heading: creativity, independence, freedom, influencing others, helping others, recognition, security, knowledge, challenging problems, status, working alone, working with people, friendships, profit, variety, excitement, tranquillity, power, competition, adventure, fast pace, detailed work, work under pressure, stability, and physical challenge. (Richard L. Knowdell, 1991.)

Now circle your most important four values from the list under the heading I always value. These values are not negotiable. You must try to find or create work that honors these four values. Your dream will probably respond to all four of them. Keep in mind, however, that values change over time. What you value when you are twenty years old will probably be different from what you value when you are thirty. Revisit this exercise periodically. Your dream should always respond to your current values.

■ Live a Typical Day

When you pick out your dream, try it out. Volunteer to work with someone doing the thing you want to do. If you cannot find anyone, at least live a typical day in your imagination. For example, say your dream is to own a tool shop. You would become a business owner. The challenges of a typical day may include learning about the business, getting permits, finding products to sell, pricing them so that people buy and you can still make a profit, sitting in the store for many hours, waiting for customers, protecting yourself from theft, etc.

Remember, no dream is perfectly glorious and fun. Every dream requires work that at times will be tedious. If you can accept the good and the bad of the work and still remain motivated, you have found your dream.

■ Commit to it

"A diamond is a piece of coal that stuck to the job." — unknown.

Now direct your energies to your dream. Imagine your success clearly. Think about it all the time. Do not delay. Do not put things off. If you waste time, if you procrastinate, you postpone your dream. Ask yourself five times every day, "what is the best thing I could do with my time right now?" That is how you recommit to your dream every day.

No matter what your dream, you should not immediately drop everything else, quit your job, completely change your life around, forget about your obligations. There is an African proverb that says, "Only a fool tests the depth of the water with both feet." If your other commitments are such that you cannot work on your dream full-time, you can start on your dream part-time. Just remember to do something with it every single day.

We must believe and act like our dream is a true possibility. Columbus had to believe that land lay toward the west before he could discover it. All Eastern-European leaders fighting for democracy had to believe that communism could be defeated. If you have read, have seen on television, or know of someone else who has done the same thing you are trying to do, then you know it is possible.

■ Keep Quiet

"If A equals success, then the formula is $A = X + Y + Z$. X is work. Y is play. Z is keep your mouth shut." — Albert Einstein.

One caution about your dream choice. Keep as quiet about it as possible. As with your purpose, you should not share your dream with just anyone.

You do not need to seek other people's opinions whether the dream you chose is right for you. Asking for opinions about your dream is like asking to borrow other people's contact lenses. They will not necessarily help you see better. In fact, they may actually injure you. Dreams are very personal.

Realize that sometimes you may have to do things that others don't like. Your family and friends may simply not understand. They may try to protect you, try to change your mind. They may be full of ideas why it is too hard, too risky, simply impossible. Ask them if they have done exactly what you are trying to do. If they have not, ignore their advice. If they have, listen carefully so you don't make the same mistakes. You must be firm with your decision to follow your dream.

If you find somebody who supports you, who is able to help you, who encourages you, you have doubled your strength. Just keep in mind that, each time you talk about your dream, you release valuable tension that is necessary to get the work done. Keep as much of the tension inside as possible.

■ Questions

1. What questions can you ask yourself to focus on your dream?
2. Do the values analysis.
3. Do you know what your dream is?

■ ■ ■

Action!

"The journey of a thousand miles begins with one step." – Lao-Tse.

You know your life's purpose, you have your dream, it is time to act. Start by first writing out all the things that must be done, from beginning to end. Then prioritize this list in order of importance. This list becomes your goals for success. Now start with item number one. Go out and do it. You may sometimes be full of fear, sometimes things won't go the way you planned them, but each action will move you closer to your dream. Whether our dream is to work for a particular company or have our own business, if we commit to it, learn what it takes to achieve it, seek the help we need, and do the work necessary, we pave our road to success.

■ Set Your Goals

"Those who do not have goals are doomed forever to work for those who do." — Brian Tracy.

There was a study done at Yale University on long-term goal-setting. Researchers interviewed the graduating class to see who had defined, written lifetime goals. Only 3 percent did. They followed up 20 years later to find that the 3 percent that had goals accomplished more in terms of career advancement and income than the remaining 97 percent combined. (Brian Tracy, 1987.)

Now that you have your dream that suits your life's purpose, goal-setting is your system for achieving it. Your goals should be written down as small, bite-size chunks of work. Some of the goals that I set for writing this book included: 1) gather research and take notes, 2) select the topics to be included in the book, 3) write for at least two hours every day, 4) learn about the publishing industry, 5) save money. My goals provided order and direction in my work. Step by step, page by page, day by day, my work began to take shape.

In many readings, I consistently found that the best way to set goals is to be very specific, describing what needs to be done physically, mentally, socially, and financially. Your goals should be reviewed often and revised as necessary. Rewarding yourself in some way as you complete each goal is highly recommended.

Set your goals in writing. Prioritize them. Complete one goal at a time. Reward yourself. Anticipate problems. Things may sometimes get chaotic and out of control, but you will be prepared.

■ Get Out of the House

"Eighty percent of success is showing up." — unknown.

Newcomers are often reluctant to mingle among Americans. They feel they won't know anybody and they're not comfortable speaking English. They decline many invitations to go places. They think they are being courteous by doing so. That's a mistake.

People are your best and most valuable resources to help you reach your goals. Networking is very important. The best way to meet more people is to simply get out of the house. Go to the library, take a class, attend church meetings, get to know more people at work, ask friends to introduce you to people they know. You will be increasing your chances of finding people who can possibly help you, encourage you, support you. They may become your customers, employers, bankers, suppliers, coaches, friends.

Many opportunities slip by because people simply don't show up to grab them. If you are invited someplace, go. Go and meet people.

■ Do the Work

"Laziness is nothing more than the habit of resting before you get tired." — Jules Renard.

Humor break:

A department manager asks one of his employees, "What do you do on Sundays?"

"Nothing," responds the employee.

"Then let me remind you that today is not Sunday."

Success is based not on what a person plans to do, but on what the person actually does. Even if you have another job and many other obligations, spend at least 7 hours per week working energetically through each of your action steps. Don't worry about the "perfect way" to do it. Don't try to be the best. Try to do your best. The results will take care of themselves.

Successful people know their work habits and idiosyncrasies. Some work better first thing in the morning. Some prefer late at night. Some prefer to work with the door closed. Some can't think creatively unless they pace back and forth. Some like to have music in the background. When are you most creative and most energized? Use this precious time and create the right environment so you can be most productive. (Benjamin J. Stein, 1994.)

■ Sometimes You Will Lose

"Expecting the world to treat you fairly because you are a good person is a little like expecting the bull not to attack you because you're a vegetarian." — Dennis Wholey.

No matter what work you do, there will probably be times when you will need something from other people. You may need their advice, recommendation, money, trust, or time. Whenever you ask for what you need, you risk the chance of being rejected. What if you are rejected by that good university, what if you don't get that job, what if you don't get that raise, what if that important customer does not buy from you? Sometimes things will seem so unfair, especially when someone else gets what you want.

If you hear the word "no," don't let it crush your enthusiasm. Stay as positive and realistic as possible. Maybe you need to change your expectations, maybe you need to try a different approach or a new idea, maybe you need to try another person, or maybe you just need to come back another day.

Experiencing rejection makes us stronger and more creative. But more than anything, it increases our chances of getting what we want. If we throw enough darts, one of them is bound to stick. We get nowhere if we lay the darts down.

It is rare that our journey to success will be easy. It will most likely be difficult, with disappointments and setbacks. When you run into trouble, analyze what happened. Were your intentions honorable? Were you prepared sufficiently? Look at what you might have done to invite the problem. When it involves your dream, another person is rarely the only cause of your trouble. Afterall, you allowed that other person close enough to do damage. Don't blame yourself or anyone else. It won't help. Instead, quickly learn from your mistakes, make adjustments, and move on.

■ Questions

1. Did you write out your action steps?
2. When are you most productive during the day?

WORK

Informational Interview

One recommended way to find out more about a particular company and to further test the type of work you would enjoy doing is to go on an informational interview. This is especially suitable if you are in college, but could be useful to anyone. An informational interview is exactly that: gathering information by talking with someone in the company. It is <u>not</u> a job interview.

If you think you would like a particular field, find out which companies in your area do that type of work. For example, if you are interested in computer programming, find someone who does this work for a living. You may know someone already or you can call a local information systems company. Ask the company's personnel department to give you the names and office phone numbers of a few computer programmers. Call them up and say that you would really appreciate learning more about their profession. Ask them if you can visit them next week for fifteen minutes. If they are too busy, ask them if they could at least answer a few questions over the telephone.

During an informational interview, you hope to learn what a <u>typical day</u> on the job is like, how the <u>industry</u> as a whole is doing, what the <u>risks of the job</u> are, what the person likes <u>most and least</u> about his work. Ask for advice on how to prepare for such a profession and where you might find other people who do that type of work. Remember, this is your chance to learn, to make sure it is what you want to do.

■ Questions:

1. What professions do you find interesting?
2. Are there companies in your area that do this type of work already?
3. Make a list of questions that you would ask during an informational interview.

■ ■ ■

Effective Job-Hunting

Once you know what type of work you want to do and for what type of company, it is time for the <u>job-hunting process</u>. This process applies to large and small companies, but it works best with small ones. Why? Because, most immigrants are pioneers who are better suited to work for smaller companies. Also, according to the U.S. Department of Labor, most jobs are being created by smaller companies.

The fastest-growing job areas will require higher levels of skill, especially administrative, managerial and technical skills. A basic knowledge and ability to use computers is a requirement at many companies. People with fluency in other languages are a big attraction. Know all this and be prepared before you even begin looking for work. If you don't have computer skills, how will you respond at the interview? If you have strong people skills, what is the best way to make them stand out?

Now, make the decision that job-hunting will be your <u>full-time job</u>, Monday through Friday, 9:00am to 5:00pm. This will put you ahead of most other job-hunters out there. If you are currently employed and want to find a new job, every spare moment should be devoted to the job search.

Many people get discouraged after one or two tries. They send out one or two resumes, go for one or two interviews, then they give up. They wait for someone to call them offering them a job. They make up their mind that it's easier to remain unemployed, or keep the job they hate. According to Richard B. Bolles, the author of *What Color is Your Parachute?*, answering advertisements in newspapers, going through employment agencies, and sending out resumes are the <u>three least effective ways</u> of finding work, and the most likely ways to generate a great deal of rejection. Don't confuse state employment agencies with <u>temporary employment companies</u>, which may be very useful in finding work, often quickly. Whatever steps you take, don't allow one or two tries to discourage you. Be mentally prepared for a process that could last at least 3 to 6 months.

So what is the <u>most effective way</u> to look for a job? The best probability of getting a job goes to the person who <u>knows his skills and who applies to a company through a referral</u>. Can you find a friend or relative who can refer you to the company that is most likely to use your skills? Try to get referred to <u>the person who has the power to hire you</u> — the boss. And be absolutely sure of what type of work you are looking for. Your friends or relatives can't help you if you don't tell them what work you want to do.

The next important step is to erase the belief that the only way to get your dream job is to show good grades in school, a lot of experience and excellent credentials. You can demonstrate to your prospective employer that you have something just as important as experience and credentials — <u>problem-solving skills</u>.

Companies need people who have experience and credentials, but they also need people who can solve problems. If you find out as much as possible about the organization before your interview and can demonstrate how you would solve a particular problem that the organization is experiencing, you will be ahead of most other candidates. Organizations may have problems with profits, advertising, staff turnover, theft, minority issues, employee effectiveness, motivation, tardiness, and many other problems.

Especially find out what problems are being faced by the person who has the power to hire you, usually the person who interviews you.

(Richard N. Bolles, 1995.) For example, the interviewer may have a problem with employees who take long lunch breaks, show up for work late, talk too much, and work too slow. By demonstrating that you will take short lunch breaks, come to work on time, stick to your work diligently, and work fast, you will be solving the problem in the mind of the interviewer. <u>Listen carefully during the interview</u>. Many problems are revealed. Talk to someone who already works for the company. Find out as much as you can. During the whole interview, relate your skills to respond to a problem that you know is heavy on the interviewer's mind.

■ Questions

1. What is the most effective way to find work?
2. How can you tie your skills to solve particular company problems?

■ ■ ■

■ The Process

Getting hired is a three-step process. Any shortcuts you take will decrease your chances of getting the job you want.

<u>Before the interview</u>, the process goes like this: you know the work you want to do, you learn about the organization you want to work for, you make the initial contact with the one individual who has the power to hire you for the job you want, and you apply directly to that person, providing him your resume. Your resume should have a job objective, your name, address, and phone number, previous job history, education, and highlights of special skills and training. (See examples of a cover letter and resume on the next few pages. There are many good books in the library that teach proper resume and cover letter preparation techniques.)

<u>When you get the interview</u>, the process is this: you practice the interview in your mind and in front of the mirror, you arrive to the interview on time dressed professionally, prepared with research on the company and what the company's potential <u>needs</u> are (don't say

the word "problems" during the interview), showing enthusiasm and professionalism, answering questions politely and briefly, presenting yourself as a resource and a solution for the company, if you feel that you want to work there. Remember, you are evaluating them as well. You should not talk about wages or salary until the employer wants you for the job and brings up the topic for discussion. Bring extra resumes with you. Maintain good eye contact. Ask a few job-related questions, but let the interviewer control the interview. A few good questions you can ask are: "What is a typical day on the job like?" and "What training programs are offered?" and "What advancement opportunities would be available in the future?"

After each interview, the process is this: you send a letter to the interviewer restating your skills and interest in the company and thanking the interviewer for his time. Many people skip this step, so if you do it, you stand out immediately. (See the example that follows.)

This three-step process may not always work. This is job-hunting, not magic. But you will succeed if you keep at it and don't take short-cuts. Remember, the person who gets hired is not always the one that is most qualified or can do the job the best. Quite often it is the person who knows most about what it takes to get hired.

As you look for work, keep in mind that the normal 9am-5pm full-time job is a rapidly fading option. Look at all possibilities — full-time, part-time, temporary, independent contractor, evening shift, etc. Any company you wish to work for is approachable, whether they are hiring or not.

■ **Questions:**

1. What steps need to be taken during the job-hunting process?
2. Do you have a resume?
3. Do you know someone who can refer you to a particular employer?
4. What questions will you ask during the interview?
5. How will you demonstrate that your skills will fit the company's needs?

(EXAMPLE OF A COVER LETTER)

Peter Salonen
15 Gateway Avenue
Littletown, VA 77035
(201) 722-5555

March 17, 1998

Ms. Amy Smith
Director
Parkway Hotels
2234 Seventh Avenue
Bigtown, VA 77055

Dear Ms. Smith:

   The Parkway Hotels always served as landmarks for me when I traveled through this country and Europe. I would like to contribute to their growth, especially their new chain, the Parkway Suites, that features reception rooms for every guest. I have enjoyed working with various types of people in my previous job experiences. Knowing that this is important to your company, I believe I would be an asset to Parkway Hotels.

   During the week of March 30, I will be visiting Bigtown and would like to speak with you concerning your training program for hotel managers. I will call you to set up a time that would be convenient for you.

   The enclosed resume outlines my education and experience.

Sincerely,

Peter Salonen

(EXAMPLE OF A RESUME)

Peter Salonen
15 Gateway Avenue
Littletown, VA 77035
(201) 722-5555

<u>Job sought</u>: Hotel Management Trainee

Skills, education and experience

<u>Working with people</u>: All the jobs I have had involve working closely with a large variety of people on many different levels. As Vice President of the Junior Class, I balanced the concerns of different groups in order to reach a common goal. As a claims interviewer with a state public assistance agency, I dealt with people under very stressful circumstances. As a research assistant with a law firm, I worked with both lawyers and clerical workers. And as a lifeguard (5 summers in Helsinki, Finland), I learned how to manage groups of people.

<u>Effective communication</u>: My campaign for class office, committee projects, and fund raising efforts (which brought in $15,000 for the junior class project), relied on effective communication in both oral and written presentations.

<u>Organization and management</u>: My participation in student government has developed my organizational and management skills. In addition, my work with the state government and a law office has made me familiar with organizational procedures.

<u>Language skills</u>: Speak fluent English and Finnish, working knowledge of German.

Chronology

<u>September 1995 to present</u>
Currently attending Ruthers College in Littletown, Virginia. Will earn a Bachelor of Arts degree in political science. Elected Vice President of the Junior Class, managed successful fund drive, directed Harvest Celebration Committee, served on many other committees, and earned 50 percent of my college expenses.

<u>January 1996 to present</u>
Work as research assistant for the law office of McCall & Brown, 980 Main Street, Littletown, Virginia 77035.

<u>September 1995 to December 1995</u>
Worked as claims interviewer intern for the Office of Public Assistance, 226 Park Street, Westrow, Virginia 77717.
Supervisor: James Fish (666) 777-5555.

<u>1990-1995</u>
Worked as a lifeguard during the summers at the Silo Pool, 2 Rue Ave., Helsinki, Finland.

Recommendations available on request.

(EXAMPLE OF A THANK YOU LETTER)

Peter Salonen
15 Gateway Avenue
Littletown, VA 77035
(201) 722-5555

April 4, 1998

Ms. Amy Smith
Director
Parkway Hotels
2234 Seventh Avenue
Bigtown, VA 77055

Dear Ms. Smith:

I really enjoyed meeting with you last Thursday and discussing the Parkway Hotels future and management training program. I am even more interested in contributing to the growth of the new Parkway Suites. I am pleased that there is a Front Desk Management position available.

Please consider my organizational skills as well as my people skills and experience, when choosing the right person for this position. If you should have any additional questions, please don't hesitate to contact me.

Thank you for your time and consideration.

Sincerely,

Peter Salonen

■ Selling Yourself

"Class is an aura of confidence, being sure without being cocky."
— Ann Landers.

Before selling any product, before asking for what you need, before most business transactions, you will be more successful if you give the other person a reason to trust you, like you, and respect you. This could be called "selling yourself." Selling yourself simply means viewing yourself as a "product" to be presented in the best possible manner. When you are job-hunting you are definitely selling yourself.

Selling yourself is a delicate matter. It requires a balance between fitting in and standing out. If you just stand out and don't fit in, people may perceive you as arrogant and dislike you. If you just fit in and don't stand out, people may like you, but may also overlook you or perceive you as less credible. The proper balance may take some time to develop and may be uncomfortable at first. Be aware of how others are perceiving you. If you are heavier on one side of the scale take small steps toward balance, without tipping the scale in the other direction.

In the section called **Relationships**, we discussed the basic steps a newcomer can take to improve acceptance among local Americans. When looking for work, it is imperative that you strive for a proper fit with the company and its employees.

■ Questions

1. What do you think you need to do to fit in as a good candidate for the job you want?
2. What do you think you need to do to stand out just enough to be hired?

■ ■ ■

■ Jobs on the Internet

We discussed the Internet in the **Education** section. The Internet is basically a worldwide network of thousands of computers. It is a great tool for learning, recreation, meeting people, advertising, and many other reasons. Many job opportunities are advertised on the Internet.

You can find individual companies listing their job openings, newspaper classified advertisements, and sites completely devoted to job-hunters (see **Sampling the Internet** in the **Appendix**). The best way to utilize the Internet, when looking for work, is to make contact with actual people, not merely posting resumes.

Whatever your interests are, there are people on the Internet with the same interests. Search them out. You can find people and companies by searching various skills, for example, <u>French language</u>. Or you can look for people from your country by searching, for example, <u>Vietnamese friends</u>. Or you can search by institutions, for example, <u>hospitals</u>. Or you can search various industries, for example, <u>healthcare</u>.

Find people that have any connection to your skills and desired career. Subscribe to newsgroups. Check out "chat-rooms," places on the Internet where people can talk online. (You may find some strange people, so be careful.) Use your E-mail (electronic mail) to contact people. If you find a particular company you like, try to find out who is in the position to hire you for the job you want. Contact that particular person.

There are many advertisements on the Internet that invite you to become an independent marketing representative or distributor. Some of these require an initial outlay of cash. Others don't. Either way, be very careful and be very certain that you want to do that type of work. Make sure the company has a good reputation. In these types of positions, you usually earn no salary until you sell something.

■ Questions:

1. What is the best way to look for a job using the Internet as a tool?
2. What are some key words or phrases that you would search for?

■　■　■

■ Large Organizations

Most people come to this country with their own firmly-held beliefs about big organizations. The goal of my parents was to work for the government. They brought this belief with them from Lithuania. At that time, Lithuania was communist-occupied and anybody who was anybody important worked for the government. What are your beliefs about big companies, small companies, government jobs, private business?

Many people, no matter where they are from, dream of working for a big corporation. We read about layoffs, stories of downsizing, stories of older people who are pushed out into early retirement, stories of women and minorities who cannot break through the "glass ceiling" (a barrier that keeps people out of high-paying upper management positions). Yet, it is still tempting to dream of being taken care of by a big company, having the security of a steady paycheck, enjoying good benefits.

It is one thing to work for a large organization in your own country. It is easier to learn the "system," the politics, the corporate culture, your language skills are strong, you have your friends, you can assess your future possibilities. When you come to this country and try to find a job with a large U.S. organization, you may not have these strengths. And some large companies don't value risk-taking, authenticity, and creativity, which are common characteristics of many new arrivals.

Should you avoid even applying for work at big companies? No. Just keep in mind that it may take 6 months to a year of filling out applications, interviewing, calling, filling out more applications, getting rejections, or not hearing anything back at all.

If you get a job with a large organization, learn as much as possible. Take the training offered and gain valuable experience. Put away as much of your salary as possible in the 401k retirement plan (see the section called **Money**). Stay with the company until you become vested in the pension plan (usually 5-7 years of full-time employment). If the work is interesting to you, stay with it. If you find yourself wishing for other work, make sure you are able to show good performance appraisals to prospective employers.

■ Small Organizations

About 80% of all businesses in America can be considered "small." Those are the businesses with 50 or less employees. They are the ones that are creating most jobs. And they are the ones that are easier to get into. If you know what it is you want to do for a living and the geographical location where you want to do it, it is not hard to find these companies. Ask people. Drive around. Go in and apply face-to-face.

The small company that hires you may not provide a pension plan for your future retirement. This is not unusual. You will need to set money aside yourself. Some strategies were outlined in the **Money** section.

■ Questions

1. Have you thought about what type of company is most suitable for your career choice and goals?
2. How will you contact the person that has the power to hire you?

■ ■ ■

■ Equal Employment Opportunity

The Equal Employment Opportunity Commission (EEOC) serves to protect employees from discrimination on the basis of race, color, religion and gender. Title VII of the Civil Rights Act of 1964 also protects individuals against employment discrimination on the basis of national origin. For example, requiring employees to speak only English or requiring job applicants to be fluent with no foreign accent may violate Title VII. The powers of EEOC usually extend to private employers with 15 or more employees, all educational institutions, state and local governments, and labor unions with 15 or more members.

During the interview process, there are questions an employer can ask, and those he cannot ask. You may have to answer questions related to your ability to perform the proposed job, but you do not have to answer personal questions related to any disabilities you have that will not interfere with your work. You may be asked to have a medical exam, but this should only be after you are offered the job. You may also be asked to go for a drug test.

If you are ever in a situation where you have been discriminated against, you can call the EEOC, ☎1-800-669-3362, to find out what you can do.

■ Diversity

In many larger organizations, there is a strong movement toward managing diversity – making the most of the variety of people available in the workforce. The concept of diversity includes age, gender, lifestyle, religion, education, and language. Although upper management circles are still often made up of white males, companies are realizing the costs associated with ignoring or devaluing different population groups. The main costs are: loss of business to certain customer types and lawsuits.

When applying for work, especially at a large organization, use the concept of diversity to create value over an American-born candidate. Emphasize your bilingual skills, cultural sensitivity to ethnic customers, networking in ethnic communities, and travel experience. It should give you some confidence to know that, all things being equal, many corporations these days would probably rather hire a "Rodriguez" instead of a "Jones."

■ Question

1. How will you emphasize your diverse background as a positive aspect to an employer?

■   ■   ■

■ Reasons For Not Getting the Job

The following are some reasons why companies do not select a particular job seeker.

- ■ No enthusiasm for the job being offered
- ■ No job goals – "I'll take any job"
- ■ Poor communication skills
- ■ Poor appearance
- ■ No knowledge about the company
- ■ Lack of employment experience

- No car of their own
- Late for the interview
- Talking too much about themselves
- Dishonesty
- Irresponsible statements or behavior

Just think what type of person you would want working for you. Any company that considers you for employment will want the best candidate. The interview will reveal all of the above. It is the deciding factor of who gets the job.

■ Question

1. Knowing the reasons why employers don't hire certain applicants, how will you prepare to improve your chances of getting the job offer?

■ ■ ■

Documentation

 You got the job! Time for the paperwork. You will need to complete Form I-9 for employment verification. You will need to show your employer various documents. The main documents accepted are a social security card, the I-94 card with employment authorization, and any Employment Authorization Document (EAD), such as the I-688B or the new I-766. You may also have to provide copies of your passport, driver's license, and other identification.

If you have a degree or other credentials from your country, that are not in English, you can contact the World Education Services, Inc., ☎1-212-966-6311, to inquire about professional translation and credentials evaluation. Your employer may request this from you. Also your country's embassy may help you with this matter.

If you are here on a student's visa (F-1), you cannot work your first year. You can start to work approximately 20 hours per week in your second year. During school vacations you are normally allowed to work full-time. After you graduate, you can usually remain in the U.S. and work up to 12 months full-time. During this time, many F-1 visa holders try to get a change of status through employer-sponsorship (to an H1B visa or permanent residency).

When you start your job, for tax purposes, your employer will have you fill out a "W-4" form. This will show the number of deductions you are claiming. The more legal deductions you have, the less taxes will be taken out. Most people claim one deduction for each family member. If your spouse also has a job, be careful not to claim too many deductions or you may owe taxes at the end of the year. (See the **Money** section for more discussion on taxes.) Before you start your job, you may also have to fill out health forms and make other benefits decisions. Your supervisor or the personnel department can help you.

If you get a job offer and are not required to show any documentation, you will probably be working "under the table." This is obviously an illegal situation. If you accept the position, expect your pay to be lower, expect to have no benefits, expect poorer working conditions, and expect no job security. The quicker you can get legal work, the better. If you don't have a legal work permit (this may be called by various names: green card, employer sponsorship, permanent residence, etc.), consult with an immigration attorney about the possibility of changing your visa status. <u>Do this before your visa expires</u>.

Learn as much as you can about the process of obtaining a <u>work permit for foreigners</u>. You will need to obtain a government publication called, *Instructions for Filing Applications for Alien Employment Certification* and *Form ETA-750, Parts A and B*. They can be requested from the U.S. Department of Labor by calling ☎1-202-219-5263. Or send your request by mail to:

Labor Certification Division
Employment & Training Administration
U.S. Department of Labor
200 Constitution Ave., NW, Room N4456
Washington, DC 20210

If you find an employer that is willing to sponsor you, the application will have to be made through the local state employment office.

This is not easy to do. It is time-consuming and frustrating. And it costs money. If you are familiar with the procedure yourself and are willing to take pay deductions to pay for all legal matters, it will be easier to find a sponsor. They will be less scared of the paperwork and more willing to go through the process.

■ **Questions**

1. What documentation do you need to be legally employed in the U.S?
2. If you don't have the proper documentation, what will you do to try to get it?

■   ■   ■

The Reality of Change

 "The factory of the future will have only two employees, a man and a dog. The man will be there to feed the dog. The dog will be there to keep the man from touching the equipment." —Warren Bennis.

It used to be the Industrial Age. Now it is the Information Age. Newcomers who are coming with manufacturing, agricultural, production and other similar labor skills, will find it harder to compete for employment. America sells information and service more than actual products. But whether you work with tractors or patients, what you know now will most likely be "historical data" next year.

Continuing your education, absorbing more and more information, gathering knowledge, improving your skills, changing with the times are minimum expectations for success in the current world of work. This cannot be done without constant reading, studying, Internet browsing, volunteering and networking, especially as they pertain to your field of work. Your employability, and thus job security, will come from your value. And your value has to be more than what you cost, whether you make $5 per hour or $50 per hour. Through observation, you will surely notice the speed of American action. They get down to business fast, the clock is always ticking, performance is what matters.

Probably many people who already have jobs will skip this entire section. If you already have a job and are still trying to learn more, congratulations! You have the right attitude!

■ Questions

1. How do you plan to continue your education?
2. What do you need to learn to increase your value as an employee?

■   ■   ■

Starting Your Own Business

"Life is pretty simple: you do some stuff. Most fails. Some works. You do more of what works. If it works big, others quickly copy it. Then you do something else. The trick is in doing something else." — Tom Peters.

It is a fact of life in America, that with each passing year, more and more people become self-employed. Many could be found delivering professional services, consulting, or a multitude of other services on a contractual basis. Others prefer to be franchise owners. And still others start a business from home.

Before going into business for yourself, you must do a lot of research and talk to other people who are doing the same thing you plan to do. Many entrepreneurs fall short in both areas and fail within the first few years. Have a clear idea of the type of business you want to start, look up businesses that are already doing that and drive over to talk to the owners. Find out the risks, the licensing and insurance requirements, the potential obstacles, and the required skills to meet daily challenges. Do you possess those skills?

Another reason why small businesses fail is lack of finances. The cost to start an average business is close to $30,000. Many entrepreneurs are finding ways to start their own businesses without this upfront cost — by <u>starting from home</u>. According to *Entrepreneur Magazine*, every 11 seconds someone starts a home-based business. The success rate is higher than outside businesses, simply due to lower financial obligations.

Immigrants to this country have proven throughout the ages that by assessing the marketplace around them, using their skills to make a difference, working smart, and persisting despite obstacles, they are able to achieve great things. As you gain experience working for an American employer, always be on the lookout for opportunities to do more for yourself. Job security in America is a thing of the past. <u>Gain experience as you work for someone else and see if the knowledge could be used to build a business for yourself</u>. Just as diversifying your investments gives your money more security, diversifying your <u>sources of income</u> does the same.

■ Turning Your Passion Into a Business

"The real tragedy in life is not being limited to one talent, but in failing to use that one talent." — Edgar Watson Howe.

At a sales seminar I once attended, I heard a story about a man who was trying to decide what he wanted to do for a living. He had jumped from job to job, hated them all, wasn't sure what his dream was, didn't know what to do. All along, however, he knew he had a skill for working with leather. It was his hobby. He especially loved making belts. He started making belts for his friends. Then he started selling them to stores. He turned his passion into a business. His wife helped him find customers and took care of the accounting. When he was asked how he felt about his work, he responded that it was like "eating candy all day long." He simply loved it.

If you have a special talent or a hobby you love, you may be able to turn it into a business. If someone else has done it, so can you. Analyze your values. Do you value creativity, independence, working alone, and profit? If you do, then you may find success as a business owner. Be creative, flexible, and start small. Don't expect much income for some time. Find people who can teach you what you don't know.

■ **Questions**

1. Why do many small businesses fail?
2. What experience and interests do you have that would be useful in your own business?

■ ■ ■

■ **Business Licensing**

Every state has its own legal requirements for business operation. With some research in the local library and talking with the local Chamber of Commerce you can find answers to most of your questions. The Small Business Administration (SBA) has a multitude of resources for the small business owner. Call the Small Business Answer Desk, ☎1-800-827-5722, and ask for a free resource guide, listing the various publications. A few are also available in Spanish.

The simplest form of business is a <u>sole proprietorship</u>. It is easy to set up. You become the business. If you operate under a company name rather than your own name, you will need to file a <u>fictitious name certificate</u>. Banks will want to see this before giving you an account in the company's name. Also you may need a <u>reseller's certificate</u>, if you wish to be exempt from taxes for items you will buy and then sell again. You may need to show this certificate to get wholesale pricing. Both certificates can usually be obtained at your state's assessment and taxation office for a small fee.

If your business requires other employees besides yourself, you will need to get a federal taxpayer identification number from the Internal Revenue Service (IRS), ☎1-800-829-1040. You will be required to withhold taxes, unemployment insurance and social security payments. Also request information and forms from the IRS to make estimated quarterly tax payments, which you may need to file, depending on your income. The state will also require regular payments of sales taxes that you collect while doing business.

Other regulations and laws may also apply, depending on your type of business. Restaurants, for example, are highly regulated. Write to the Occupational Safety and Health Administration (OSHA) for information on mandatory responsibilities and safety standards for your type of business:

OSHA— Information Office
U.S. Department of Labor
200 Constitution Ave., N.W. Rm. S2315
Washington, DC 20210

Libraries, the Internet, bookstores, the Department of Labor, and the Small Business Administration are full of valuable information about how to run a small business. You will need a lot of assistance before you start. Get all the permits, licenses, certificates in order. Keep records and receipts of everything you buy, everything you sell, everywhere you go. Consult with professionals in your field to minimize mistakes.

■ Question

1. What licenses does your business require?

■ ■ ■

■ Creating Value

Humor break:
A strong man comes to a construction company looking for work.
"What can you do?" the manager asks.
"I could dig."
"And what else can you do?"
"I could also not dig."

People pay for the services or products which they value. If your company provides value that is superior to what your competitors provide, people will pull out their wallets. There are two types of values in business. There is <u>real value</u> and <u>perceived value</u>. Both are equally important. Let me illustrate this with the following example.

Two girls, named Brigita and Laura, work in a candy store. Brigita always has a long line of children waiting to buy from her. Laura is noticeably less busy. The owner asks one of the boys in Brigita's line why he wants to buy from her and not the other girl. The boy responds, "Brigita gives us more." The owner stands back and watches the two girls work. Laura pours a lot of candy in a bag, weighs it, and then keeps taking some out to measure a pound. Brigita, on the other hand, pours a little bit in the bag, weighs it, and keeps adding and adding until she reaches a pound. The <u>real value</u> was a pound of candy, but Brigita sold it with greater <u>perceived value</u>.

A person's perception becomes his reality. If I perceive that I am getting less than I deserve, I will buy from someone else. The place I did not buy from will never know why they lost the sale. One lost sale after another can threaten the survival of the business. That is why it is so important, as a person or as a business, to create value.

▪ Questions

1. Think of some other examples of real and perceived value.

2. How can your business create more value over your competitors?

▪ ▪ ▪

▪ Tale of Two Managers

"By working faithfully eight hours a day, you may eventually get to be a boss and work twelve hours a day." — Robert Frost.

As your business grows, you may have to hire and supervise other people. The following story describes two types of managerial styles – one effective, one not.

There once were two sales managers that worked for the same company, supervised the same number of people, and reported to the same director. Their business pressures, time constraints, and goals were similar. They were both hard workers. How the managers differed was in the way they treated their team members. One manager treated each person on his team like a loser, while the other manager treated each person on his team like a winner. This made a huge impact on performance results.

The first manager always made sure that people knew who was "the boss." He withheld information to control people, asked for meaningless reports, expected an explanation for every activity, always demanded that things be done a certain way, and rarely had a genuinely kind word for anyone. His actions created insecurity, fear, anger, and crushed enthusiasm. His team's sales plummeted.

The second manager found something great about all team members and reminded them at every opportunity of each particular strength. If he had to correct something an employee did wrong, he would preface it with genuine examples of what that employee did right. Sometimes he would just skip over and not comment on a mistake and, purely by omission, the person understood the error. He tried to do what the Japanese have done for decades — protect the person's dignity. He emphasized the importance of teamwork, risk-taking, excellence, and fun. His team was one of the highest performing teams in the company.

What is the moral of this story? How you treat your employees will come back to either haunt you or bless you. The best way to look after your own interests is to genuinely look after the interests of the people who work for you. True leaders know this.

■ Questions

1. Will your business require the help of employees?
2. How prepared are you to manage other people?

■ ■ ■

■ Basics of Marketing

Humor break:
One clever business owner hung a sign on his restaurant's door: "Here we produce with love!"

After a few hours his competitor hung this sign on his restaurant's door: "Here we produce with butter!"

Some newcomers to America may view the concept of marketing with skepticism or distaste. Perhaps profit-making was viewed negatively in their countries. Even if you don't agree with the concept, it is important to understand it.

Marketing is simply the process of producing, pricing, promoting, and distributing a product or service. Usually, the purpose of marketing is to gain a profit, but it doesn't have to be. Non-profit organizations such as churches and charities still need to follow some marketing basics to stay alive.

To have any profits, even if we are the only person that provides the product or service, we need to maximize all the elements of marketing. Good marketing requires that you know your product and quality of service very well. You need to know why some people buy from you, and why other people don't. For example, if you have a pizza restaurant, and you want to increase your clientele, it is silly to speculate, "if I add more cheese, more people will come." You must satisfy your customers according to their wishes, not your guesses. You may think they want more cheese, but they may actually want dimmer lights for romance.

The most difficult job of marketing, and where companies often fail, is in finding out who their customer is, what he wants, and what is the best way to give him what he wants. Companies must know current customer desires and must anticipate changes in those desires.

So who is the boss? Well, you make the pizza, it is your restaurant, your chairs and tables, you pay the rent, you hire the people, you must be the boss! No, you are not. The customer is always the <u>real boss</u>. Businesses that adopt the right mentality and learn how to delight their customers increase their chances of survival tremendously.

The elements of marketing effect every individual in the world. Each person sometime during his life, will be both, a customer of a product or service and a provider of a product or service. With knowledge of marketing concepts, every personal and business transaction can achieve a more favorable outcome.

■ Question

1. What areas of marketing do you need to develop for your business?
2. What are your feelings about sales and profit-making?

■ ■ ■

■ Negotiation Reminders

We discussed in the **Major Purchases** section that "you don't get what you deserve, you get what you negotiate." As a reminder, negotiation is communication with a purpose for a win/win agreement — you win and the other person wins. Negotiation skills are valuable to everyone. You will need them especially if you have your own business. You may need to negotiate with buyers, suppliers, banks, lawyers, with people at varied professional and educational levels.

The main thing to remember is that most decisions in business are not about people, they are about things. You can become a successful negotiator by confronting the things or the problem, never the people. See yourself as a partner not an opponent. Build a bridge, not a wall. Negotiation is similar to a marriage. If one side loses, the other side will not win either. (Roger Fisher, 1981.)

When negotiating for anything have a plan, focus on the other person's interests, and provide some options. If the person you are negotiating with becomes stubborn or hostile or simply lies to you, continue to negotiate. Don't respond with the same attitude. Ask for suggestions from the person to soften him up and look for an option that is good for both of you. There is a saying that sums up this strategy: "when a dog runs at you, whistle for him." Do not respond with threats or be hostile yourself. Do not act inferior or superior. Have an alternative in mind so that if negotiations fail, you can simply walk away. And always remember: never accept a "no" answer from someone who could not give you a "yes" from the very beginning. Talk to the right person.

■ Questions

1. How much experience do you have in negotiating with people?
2. What might you have to negotiate for in your business?

■ To Be an Entrepreneur

If you have what it takes, having your own business could be a truly rewarding experience. Always remember that the longer you are in it, the bigger you get, the more humble you have to become, and the more help you must give to others. I will close this section with the official Credo of the American Entrepreneurs Association, which is applicable to all pioneers:

> *"I do not choose to be a common person. It is my right to be uncommon—if I can. I seek opportunity—not security. I do not wish to be a kept citizen, humbled and dulled by having the state look after me. I want to take the calculated risk, to dream and to build, to fail and to succeed. I prefer the challenges of life to the guaranteed existence: the thrill of fulfillment to the stale calm of Utopia. I will not trade my freedom for beneficence nor my dignity for a handout. I will never cower before any master nor bend to any threat. It is my heritage to stand erect, proud and unafraid; to think and act for myself, to enjoy the benefit of my creations and to face the world boldly and say: This with God's help, I have done. All this is what it means to be an Entrepreneur."*

In pursuing the work you want to do, you become an entrepreneur. Whether you work for yourself, work for someone else, stay home with the kids, it doesn't matter. Your work is your corporation and becomes what you make of it.

■ Questions

1. Do you have the right attitude to become an entrepreneur?
2. What skills do you still need to develop?
3. Where will you get the education and experience to develop those skills?

HEALTH, SAFETY AND OTHER TIPS

Health Tips

■ Healthcare

In the U.S., every person is responsible for paying for health services. Because healthcare is very expensive, most people rely on insurance programs, usually through their employer. Health insurance can be obtained for a monthly payment. Some employers pay a part of that payment. There could be a waiting period from the time you are hired until you become eligible for health insurance.

There are many insurance companies offering different types of programs. Health maintenance organizations (usually called HMOs) are an increasingly common form of insurance program. Through this system, care is provided by a group of private doctors and clinics. Each member of an HMO has an assigned doctor who provides primary care and must approve any visits to emergency rooms, hospitals, or specialists. In some situations, the full cost of medical care will be paid by the insurance company. In other cases, you will be required to pay part of the costs. (See the **Major Purchases** section for more discussion on health insurance.)

In most cases, an appointment is required for medical, dental, or mental healthcare. Emergency rooms do not require an appointment. They are usually located in hospitals and should be used only when absolutely necessary, for sudden and extreme health problems.

■ If You Can't Afford Healthcare

To assist people with low incomes, there are government programs which cover some medical expenses. Medicaid is one such program. Applicants must complete forms that require proof of income and other personal information.

An informed person will seek out any available free medical products or services. When I was a college student with no dental insurance and wisdom teeth that had to come out, I enrolled in a clinical study at the National Institutes of Health and was able to get my wisdom teeth out for free. If you are faced with an illness that requires expensive medications or procedures, consider clinical trials as a way to obtain the care that you need, but cannot afford. Your doctor may know of some ongoing studies.

When it comes to purchasing prescribed drugs, brand name medicines are usually much more expensive than generic medicines. Ask your doctor or pharmacist if a generic equivalent is available for the drug you need. If you will need to be on a specific medication for a long period of time, consider purchasing the drugs from a mail-order pharmacy. Go to the library and look through the *Consumer Reports* for a listing and evaluation of mail-order pharmacies. One very popular mail-order service is the American Association of Retired Persons (AARP), ☎1-800-456-2277. They fill over 10 million prescriptions every year. Anyone can use them, not just retired people.

If you don't have prescription drug coverage as part of your health insurance plan and fall below a certain income level, most major pharmaceutical companies will provide free prescribed drugs necessary to treat your condition. Most people do not know this. In brief, this is the process to obtaining free prescription drugs:

■ When your doctor prescribes you a medication, always ask for free samples. Many drug companies provide free samples of their brand name drugs. They want doctors to try them out on a few patients, to find them useful, and then to prescribe them.

■ Whether the doctor has any free samples or not, ask for the name of the pharmaceutical company that makes the drug. Make sure you know the correct name of the drug you are prescribed. Your doctor or any pharmacist should be able to provide the phone number and address of most drug companies. They are all listed in the Manufacturer's Index of the *Physician's Desk Reference* (PDR), owned by most doctors.

■ Call the company that makes your drug and ask for the address and phone number of their "indigent patient program." Some companies call it by different names, such as the "patient assistance program."

■ Call the number you are given and ask for an application. It is even smarter to have the application faxed directly to your doctor (have the fax number ready before you call the indigent patient program). Your doctor will have to fill out a portion of the form and will do it faster if it is faxed. You will have to fill out the rest of the form. Send the form to the address on the application.

■ If you qualify for free medicine, it will be sent directly to your doctor within 2-3 weeks. You can then go and pick it up.

This arrangement is especially useful for chronic medications, drugs you have to take for a long time. Some people spend their food money on medicine because they don't know how to take advantage of these programs.

As a general guideline, get a second opinion if any major illness is diagnosed by your physician. Before any medical procedure, ask your doctor or the hospital how much it is going to cost. Then ask for a reduced-payment plan, where you can pay on a monthly basis until the bill is settled.

■ Immunization Information

Immunizations are very important to protect your children from many types of disease. Consult your physician regarding the schedule below:

<u>Polio (OPV)</u> – 2, 4, 6 months and 4-6 years.

<u>Diphtheria-Tetanus-Pertussis (DTP, DTaP)</u> – 2, 4, 6, 15 months and 4-6 years. Also a tetanus-diphtheria (Td) shot at 15 years.

<u>Measles-Mumps-Rubella (MMR)</u> – 12-15 months and 4-6 years, or 11-12 years.

<u>Haemophilus influenzae</u> type b (Hib) – 2, 4, 6 and 12-15 months, or 2, 4 and 12-15 months, depending on vaccine type.

<u>Hepatitis B (HBV)</u> – birth, 1-2 months and 6-18 months, or 1-2 months, 4 months and 6-18 months.

<u>Chickenpox (VZV)</u> – 12-18 months.

Source: U.S. Department of Health and Human Services, 1996

■ Warning Signs of Depression

We all feel "down" at times. However, if these feelings are very strong or last for a long time, they may be due to a medical illness called depression. Every year, about 10% of the American population suffers from a depressive illness. A serious loss, chronic illness, difficult relationship, financial problem, or any unwelcome <u>change in life patterns</u> (common for immigrants and refugees) can trigger a depressive episode.

This illness can be treated, but it is often not recognized by patients and clinicians. If you have four or more of the warning signs listed below, be sure to talk with your physician.

<u>Warning signs of depression:</u>
- Feeling sad, hopeless or guilty
- Loss of interest and pleasure in daily activities

- Sleep problems (either too much or too little)
- Fatigue, low energy, or feeling "slowed down"
- Problems making decisions or thinking clearly
- Crying a lot
- Changes in appetite or weight (up or down)
- Thoughts of suicide or death

Source: U.S. Department of Health and Human Services, 1996

■ Questions

1. What are some types of health insurance plans that are available to you?
2. What are some low-cost or free medical care options?

■ ■ ■

Safety Tips

■ Emergencies

One of your first goals in America should be to prepare yourself and your family for emergency situations. If your English is limited, you need to learn and practice what to say and what to do. If your problem is very serious — a robber trying to break in, your house is on fire, your mother is having a heart attack — always dial 911 on your telephone. Know how to describe what is happening. If you cannot explain the problem in English, just say "Help" or "Emergency" and <u>do not</u> hang up the telephone. The open phone line will indicate where you are.

■ Police

In some countries, a police officer can pull someone over for no reason. In the U.S., a police officer has to have a specific reason or suspicion of wrongdoing, before he can stop your car.

As you are driving, if you see an officer point to your car and motion you to pull to the side or if he follows you in his car with his lights on, pull the car to the right side of the road and stop. Stay in your car. Don't get out, unless asked by the police officer. The officer may come over and may ask for your driver's license, registration, and insurance papers. Have all the documents with you, be polite, and do as you are told. Don't argue. Be polite. He may have stopped you because you were driving too fast. He first wants to establish that you have a driver's permit, that the car is yours or you have permission to drive it, and that the car is insured. On rare occasions, in a few select states, such as California, the officer may also ask for your immigration papers.

If you have problems understanding the officer, say "I am new to America, can you please speak slowly." The officer may take your documents back to his car and come back a few minutes later. He will explain why he stopped you and may give you a piece of paper. This could be a "warning" that does not need to be paid or a "ticket," a fine that you need to pay within a certain number of days.

If it's a moving violation and you pay the ticket, you may be assessed points against your license. Points may increase your insurance costs. If you appeal the ticket, you will be scheduled a court date to plead your case. The courts cannot force you to testify against yourself. You do not have to admit you were at fault. If you get a parking ticket, it often saves time and frustration to just pay the ticket. Unpaid parking tickets can lead to "booting" of your car. The car is immobilized until your fines are paid up.

Remember that in the U.S., if you are accused of a crime, you are considered innocent until proven guilty. You have a right to an attorney who will represent you in court. If you cannot afford an attorney, the court will appoint one to represent you.

■ Car Accident

If you are ever involved in a car accident, stop your car as soon as it is safe to do so. Try to get out of the flow of traffic if possible. Stay inside or by your car. Do not leave. Ask someone to call the police, even for a minor accident. Many people have car phones and would be willing to do so.

Even if you caused the accident, <u>most experts recommend that you do not admit that it was your fault</u>. Don't say you are sorry and don't accuse the other person. Say as little as possible. Get the name, address, phone number, insurance company, and driver's license number of the other person involved in the accident. Also write down the year, make, model and license number of the other car.

The other person involved in the accident is also entitled to the same information from you. If the car is not yours, provide the name and phone number of the owner. If there were any witnesses to the accident, get their name, address and phone number. When the police officer arrives, answer his questions. Get the officer's name, phone number and the police report number. Notify your insurance company as soon as possible.

If you feel that you have been hurt, you should go to the hospital or your doctor the same day of the accident.

■ Crime: If They Want What You Have

Give it to them. If a perpetrator is simply after your money or your car or your purse, <u>comply immediately</u>. Give him what he wants. Be polite, never hostile. Don't make any sudden moves. Make sure you have something to give him. He may get angry if he gets nothing.

Approximately 25,000 carjackings occur each year (Business Driver, 1996). A carjacking is a forceful takeover of your vehicle. Carjackings could occur at gas stations, at red lights, in parking lots, just about anywhere. Carjackers often bump an innocent driver at a red light. When the driver gets out to inspect his car, they make their attack. If you didn't hear screeching tires, as if a car is trying to come to an immediate stop, do not get out. Signal the other car to follow you to a safe place to exchange information. Always keep your car doors locked and windows rolled up. As you are driving along, if you believe you are being followed, keep driving to a well-lit public place or a police station. <u>Do not drive to your home</u>.

If you see a car accident up ahead as you are driving, it is not recommended that you stop to help out. Carjackers and other perpetrators use this method to lure people. It is better to drive to a pay phone to call for assistance.

Sometimes when a wallet is stolen, it is only for the cash inside. But more and more often it is stolen for an identity. If a thief steals your wallet or purse and finds credit cards, a driver's license, and checkbook, they could be in business using your name for many months. Even if you notify the banks and cancel all accounts, the thief quite often can open new accounts, leaving unpaid bills, overdrawn checks, doing your credit history a lot of damage.

If you find yourself with a lost or stolen wallet, cancel all your credit accounts by calling the banks and department stores, file a police report, and notify the three credit bureaus that fraud is possible. The telephone numbers are as follows: Experian — ☎1-800-422-4879, Equifax — ☎1-800-525-6285, and Trans Union — ☎1-800-680-7289.

■ Crime: If They Want YOU

Two sources of major terror in America are the high rates of child abduction and rape. You must teach your children to take all precautions possible. Teach them and practice with them how to fight, bite, run, and hide from a predator. Teach them to be able to scream out "This is not my dad!" People see many incidents between parents and misbehaving children. If your child is being abducted and only appears to cry or struggle, that will not be enough to draw attention.

If a perpetrator is after <u>you</u>, the place where you are originally attacked is where you must get away. Even if you are threatened with a gun, for example, to keep quiet and to get into a car, according to many safety experts, <u>you must not be taken to the second location</u>. Chances of surviving the second location are very slim. Do everything possible to get away at the first location, where you are first approached.

Before you move to a new neighborhood, find out which areas are considered "bad" by most people. As a general precaution, keep your doors locked at all times, in your car and in your home. Don't open the door carelessly, if you don't know the person knocking.

Write your address close to each phone in the house, so you and your children can quickly read it to the police when you dial 911 in the event of an emergency.

■ **Scams**

There is a famous saying in America — "there is no such thing as a free lunch." Anything that may appear too wonderful, probably is too wonderful to be true.

What is a scam? It is an act of swindling or tricking someone out of their money. Many scams are specifically targeted at foreigners, who usually do not know any better. The best precaution to take is to never give your credit card number, bank account number, address, or social security number over the telephone, unless you are making the call and are familiar with the company or person.

Don't be rushed into buying anything. If you feel pressured or uncomfortable, get out of the situation quickly. Don't respond to any postcards that say you won a prize. This usually means that you have to buy something to get your "free" prize or travel a long distance to listen to a presentation and get a cheap prize. Don't dial any "900" numbers. They will cost you plenty. Also don't dial any "809" numbers (unless you are specifically initiating a call to the Carribean). This is a new scam identified by the National Fraud Information Center. The crooks try to keep you on the phone for as long as possible and all you will get is an expensive phone bill.

It is incredible how many legitimate businesses exist that, in the name of profit, carry on practices that consistently defraud or trick customers into paying more than they would if they <u>knew better</u>. Become a customer that knows better. Check the *Consumer Reports* publications. Shop around. When buying insurance, a car, a bed, a computer, medical services, home improvement services, or anything major, always get at least three price quotes. Pay with a credit card whenever possible. Get receipts as proof of payment.

■ **Your Signature**

Avoid signing anything, unless you fully understand what you are signing and the implications of your signature. Point to words you don't understand and say, "please explain." Ask, "what else do I need to know about this?" and "by when can I cancel and get my money back?"

A signature on the back of a check is as good as cash. If you have to send any endorsed (signed) checks through the mail, add the words "For Deposit Only" above your signature on the back of each check.

■ Important to Make Copies

Make copies of everything. You should have copies of your passport, driver's license, immigration papers, car registration, and any important documents. Before you part with an important piece of paper, make a copy of it. You can make copies at libraries, copy centers, supermarkets, postal service centers, just about anywhere. You should also make extra keys for your apartment and car. Most hardware stores provide this service.

■ Questions

1. What precautions can you take to avoid crime?
2. What will you do in the event of an emergency?

■ ■ ■

Miscellaneous Tips

■ American Laws That May Differ from Laws in Your Country

✓ In many places in the U.S., it is illegal to smoke in public places such as theaters or offices. In other places, such as restaurants, people who smoke must remain in designated areas.

✓ It is illegal to purchase, sell, or use narcotics or other addictive drugs and controlled substances.

✓ It is illegal to drive a car if you do not have a U.S. driver's license or if you have been drinking alcohol.

✓ Many states have laws regarding the safety of children in automobiles. For example, special safety seats are required for infants and seatbelts for children and adults.

✓ Physical abuse of your spouse or your child is illegal.

✓ Sex with minors (under 18 years of age in most states) is illegal.

✓ Offensive comments or behavior of a sexual nature in the workplace (sexual harassment) is illegal.

✓ Males between the ages of 18 and 25 must register with the Selective Service, an agency which can call individuals for military service, usually in time of war. All male lawful permanent residents, refugees, parolees, and asylum-seekers must register within 30 days of their 18th birthday or within 30 days of their arrival in the U.S., if age 18 through 25. Most post offices have the required form for registration (SSS Form 1M). At present, all members of the U.S. armed forces are volunteers, so registration <u>does not</u> mean enlisting in the armed forces. Failure to register may be cause for denial of permanent residency (green card) and citizenship. Lawfully admitted nonimmigrant aliens (for example, those on visitor or student visas) are not required to register.

✓ In most places, it is not legal to hunt game or fish without a license, and you must learn and obey other laws relating to these activities.

✓ Basic freedoms, such as freedom of speech, freedom of religion, and freedom of assembly are protected for everyone in the U.S.

✓ It is not appropriate to give money or tips to a police officer or any government official as thanks for assistance.

✓ If you hold refugee status, you cannot return to your country of origin or you may not be permitted to reenter the United States.

■ Immigration Overview

Entire books have been written describing the specifics of immigration. Many become outdated soon after publication. Being that each individual's case is different and there are so many variables and constant changes, you will need to obtain accurate, up-to-date information that specifically applies to you. This is best done with the assistance of a qualified immigration attorney.

Information and forms can also be obtained by calling or visiting your local Immigration and Naturalization Service (INS) office. The address and phone number can be found in the phonebook. You can also contact the Central INS Office, 425 I Street, N.W., Washington, DC 20536, ☎1-202-514-4316. Or if you know the forms you need, dial ☎1-800-870-3676 to order them for free.

Upon arrival to the U.S., you were issued an I-94 card. It is a small, white 3x5 card that is referred to as an "entry permit" and shows your name, date and place of birth, and date of entry into the U.S. If you are admitted for permanent residence, it will also contain an INS file number (the "A" number). The I-94 is an important document. Make a copy and carry only the copy with you. Keep the original in a safe place, only taking it out for official purposes.

Some strict immigration rules have taken effect in 1997. Some of the most important ones are: 1) you have only one year from the date of your arrival to apply for political asylum; 2) you will be barred from returning to the United States for three years if you stay more than 180 days after the expiration date on your I-94 (not the date on your visa) and barred from returning for ten years if you stay more than one year; 3) new regulations allow INS agents to refuse a refugee's entry at the airport, if the refugee does not have proper documentation and cannot demonstrate a credible fear of persecution if returned back to his homeland. Many refugees cannot articulate this properly and are turned away.

A green card is a document that establishes you as a lawful permanent resident of the U.S. It is your authorization to work. It gives you more freedom to travel and to bring your spouse and unmarried children to the U.S. (When you obtain your citizenship, you can also petition for your parents to come over.)

▪ Immigration Lawyers

Depending on your status, it is highly recommended that you consult with an experienced immigration lawyer. There is an association called the American Immigration Lawyers Association (AILA). Most lawyers specializing in immigration law belong to this association. It is best to be referred by someone who has used a local lawyer's services but you may also contact AILA, ☎1-202-371-9377. They maintain a list of all member attorneys within each state. The first visit with a lawyer is often free.

■ Citizenship

You are usually able to apply for U.S. citizenship after five years of permanent residency (3 years, if you marry a U.S. citizen). You will be expected to prove your knowledge of U.S. history and government and will have to demonstrate your ability to speak English. Citizenship gives you a right to vote in elections and to hold public office. It also gives you the right to petition to the INS on behalf of your parents to obtain an immigrant visa for them, as well as on behalf of your adult children and your brothers and sisters, as long as you are at least 21 years old. (The green card, or permanent residency, only allows for your spouse and unmarried children.)

■ Social Security Administration

The Social Security Administration (SSA) issues three types of social security cards: 1) the usual card, valid for work, listing the person's name and number, issued to U.S. citizens and permanent residents, 2) a temporary card that is not valid for work but can be used for identification, banking, etc., issued to foreigners, 3) a temporary card that is valid for work with INS authorization. The SSA tracks each individual's earnings so it can determine future retirement or disability benefits for the individual and his dependents. It is against the law to use someone else's social security card. To obtain a card of your own, call ☎1-800-772-1213 for more information and for the address of your local SSA office.

■ Using the Telephone

You may notice that just about wherever you call, you are prompted by a recorder to press certain buttons on your phone for more information. Often the recorder will ask you to press the "pound" sign. That is the # button on the bottom right of your telephone keypad. The "asterisk" sign is the * sign on the bottom left. Some telephone numbers are written as letters, for marketing purposes. The letters simply correspond to numbers on your telephone.

You will notice that most Americans have a telephone with an answering machine. It is very customary to leave a message if you cannot get hold of someone. In fact, most people would prefer that you leave a message, so they could call you back at their convenience. Some may even be at home when you call, but prefer to let the answering machine take a message. Some newcomers resist in talking to an answering machine and prefer to keep calling back. This could be annoying to people. It is best that you get in the habit of just leaving a simple message, for example: "This is Peter calling, please call me back at 555-456-7890."

The easiest way to obtain a local telephone number is by using your local phonebook. You will notice that there is a residential phone directory and a business directory (often called the "yellow pages"). You may also dial 411 for directory assistance within your area. This is free from most public payphones.

For long-distance directory assistance, dial the area code for the city and 555-1212. (If you don't know the area code for a particular city, dial 411 and the operator will give it to you.) So, for example, if you want to get the phone number for the Kenya Embassy in Washington, DC, you would dial ☎1-202-555-1212. The operator would give you the local number. There is a charge of about 85 cents that will appear on your phone bill. If you are looking for a phone number for a major corporation or any other major agency or institution, it is best to dial ☎1-800-555-1212. This is toll-free (no cost) to you and you don't even have to know where the agency or company is located. You can just say "I need the eight-hundred number for Hyatt Hotels."

When you move into your own residence, you will need to select a long-distance carrier for your phone service. Common carriers are AT&T, MCI, and Sprint, but there are many others. The Federal Communications Commission (FCC) has authorized a new monthly charge for customers who have not chosen a long-distance carrier. To verify which company is your long-distance carrier, call ☎700-555-4141. There is no charge for the call.

There are four time zones in the United States. When it is 9:00am in Los Angeles, it is 10:00am in Denver, 11:00am in Chicago, and

12:00pm in Washington, D.C. When calling long-distance, it helps to know what time you are trying to reach someone.

■ Finding an Apartment

Many newcomers stay with relatives or friends. When it comes time to get your own apartment, you will need to pass a credit history check, pay a security deposit of one to two months rent and sign a lease. The lease is a legal and binding document. You can't just move out whenever you feel like it, without losing your security deposit and perhaps paying additional penalties. You need to give your landlord notice of when you plan to leave.

When you rent an apartment, you become a tenant or lessee. The person or company you rent from is the landlord or lessor. The local laws govern the agreements and disputes between tenants and land-lords. In the lease, you will agree to the number of people that will live in the apartment, the date the rent is due, that the apartment will be kept clean, and the number of months you agree to stay (usually 12 months minimum).

You can find an apartment through friends, co-workers, advertise-ments in the local newspaper, and real estate companies. You may be able to find a landlord from your own country, however, that does not guarantee the best conditions or the lowest price. It is common for newcomers to be taken advantage of by their own people.

A rental apartment generally includes a kitchen with a stove, sink and refrigerator. You will usually have a living room, dining room, one or two bathrooms and one or more bedrooms. The monthly rent may include electricity, heat, water, gas, and trash removal. In some cases you may be required to pay separately for these items, called utilities. Find out what is included before signing the rental agreement.

■ Tipping

In many countries, tipping is viewed strictly as a voluntary activity. You want to tip, you can. You don't want to, you don't have to. That is not the case in America. Even though tipping is made on a discretion-ary basis, it is expected. Get used to tipping whenever it is expected, especially if the service was good.

Waiters and bartenders usually get 15% of the total bill. One easy way to figure out an approximate 15% is this formula: " ? x 7 = bill." What number times 7 will equal the bill? If your meal cost $35, then $5 times 7 equals $35. You leave a $5 tip.

Doormen, room service, valet parking, and coat-check employees usually get $1. Bellmen that carry your bags to your hotel room usually get $1 per bag. Chambermaids, $1 per day.

Your hair stylist also expects to be tipped. A simple haircut, $2. A permanent or hair color, $5 and up. Being stingy with tipping will hurt the service you will receive in the future. People will remember you.

■ Traveling

Travel deals and scams are plentiful. Pay by credit card whenever possible. If the airline goes bankrupt or cancels your flight, your money has not been spent. When making reservations at a hotel, don't call the toll-free reservations number for the hotel chain. It is a sure way to overpay. The toll-free number will always quote the most expensive rooms. Call the local hotel directly, even if the call is not free. Ask for the best rate available. When you arrive, ask for even a lower rate. You may not get it. But then again you may. Hotels offer weekend rates, which are often the lowest.

Sign up for all the Frequent Flier plans you want. They are free. Inquire about them as you check in for a flight or as you make your reservation. As you accumulate miles, you may be entitled to discounts or free trips.

If you will be traveling longer than a few days and no one will be at home, interrupt newspaper deliveries and have your mail held at the post office. Leave a light on in your home, unplug appliances and computer equipment.

■ Your Community's Publications

It is unfortunate that some newcomers from my country do not subscribe or even show an interest in any of the publications put out by the American-Lithuanian community. That's somewhat narrow-minded. Subscribing to one or two publications from your country's community is important. These publications are usually not expensive and contain information on local business and social activities, job listings, discounted airfare to your country, credit unions, and various products and services. They keep you connected and give you an American perspective of what is going on in your homeland. Most articles are written and edited by highly-qualified individuals with a strong devotion to their heritage. To find out about all the publications available, contact your country's embassy.

■ **Questions**

1. What are some laws in the U.S. that differ from the laws in your country?

2. What steps are you taking to strengthen your immigration status?

SUCCESS AND SATISFACTION

Those Rebellious Foreigners!

 It's no secret that immigration is a controversial topic in America. The discussion doesn't just circle around politics or economics. Some people claim that the quality of the immigrant has changed. They say that immigrants used to come to the U.S. with big dreams, business skills, a strong work ethic. Now, some say, many come with a poor attitude. They want to be taken care of. They act like America owes them something. Even foreign-born U.S. citizens call many newcomers as "rebellious, refusing to fit in." How do these opinions apply to you? Whether you will be successful in your new life greatly depends on the answer to that question.

This section will discuss success and satisfaction. The ideas presented are, of course, influenced by American culture. This does not mean that everyone you meet in America will believe and behave this way. Many won't. And maybe some of these ideas simply do not interest you. However, if your goal is to achieve success and happiness in America, the ideas presented here are a good starting point.

The goal of this topic is to help minimize regrets, as is poignantly summarized in the following poem.

> *"Across the fields of yesterday,*
> *He sometimes comes to me*
> *A little lad just back from play –*
> *The boy I used to be.*
> *He looks at me so wistfully*
> *When once he's crept within;*
> *It is as if he hoped to see*
> *The man I might have been."*

– unknown

Personal Reflection

"If I am not for myself, who will be for me? If I am not for others, who am I for? And if not now, when?" — The Talmud.

Whatever country we are raised in, as we grow from childhood to adolescence, we are greatly influenced by our parents, school, society, and friends. As we reach adulthood, we realize that some of the influence helps us, some does not. It is up to us to continue our own development and make corrections where necessary. Making those corrections is the root of <u>new thoughts and actions</u>. In order to move forward we have to know <u>who</u> we are first.

Part of pioneer duty is to get to know yourself by honestly reflecting on your own experience and how you think other people see you. Why do it? Why take the time? Why not just live and see what happens? Because by ignoring who you are, you float along with what you have always been doing, or jump on the wave that happens to be popular with people around you.

Without self-knowledge people become easily swayed. In a new country, with so many new influences, so many possible directions, so many uncertainties, we are often tempted to follow others. We try to fulfill other people's expectations. Of course, in the long-term, this will not allow us to achieve our <u>own full potential</u>. We will end up living someone else's life, not our own.

To learn more about yourself, start by looking at what you have experienced so far in your life. Do this <u>without</u> viewing coming to America as a major personal achievement. Coming to America does not pardon or vindicate you from all your past troubles. Honestly look at yourself. Do good or bad things generally happen to you? Are you healthy? What are your good and bad habits? How do you handle stress? What do you feel you are always right about? Would you want to have a best friend that was a lot like you, that did the things you do, that said the things you say?

Also look at yourself in the mirror and ask about your commitment to be here. Do you have the "if it doesn't work out, I'll just go back" mentality? What old thoughts and behaviors have you brought with you that could hurt your chances in America?

Then try seeing yourself through the eyes of other people around you. How do people react to you? Do they seem to trust you or mistrust you? What do people praise you about? What do different people criticize you about? No matter how you see yourself, depending on your appearance and mannerisms, people may perceive you as "different." Maybe in the eyes of a native American, you obviously look like a foreigner, even before you open your mouth to speak. How does that make you feel and behave? What word would people choose to describe you – confident, shy, nice, active, slow, angry, friendly?

If American English was not your first language and you were over 13 years of age when you first came to America, you will probably speak with an accent that will be noticeable to most native Americans. That includes almost all newcomers, even people from English-speaking countries. Unless you speak <u>American English</u>, people will notice it. We came over when I was 10, I have been speaking English for 25 years, and still words will come out of my mouth that just don't sound "American." No matter how long you live in this country, certain situations may come up that will make you feel like a foreigner. How will you handle it?

Reflect on how you see yourself and how others see you. Asking yourself some questions could open your eyes to who you were in the past and who you are today. It should also give you an idea of who you will be tomorrow, if your thoughts and habits are deeply ingrained.

■ **Questions**

1. What are some of your achievements?
2. Have you asked yourself some tough questions?

■ ■ ■

Success

 Success. What a wonderful word! Everyone wants success, but few attain it. Culture and upbringing certainly influence how success is defined, but many people simply don't know what success specifically means to them. And yet, it is so closely linked to happiness.

If you define success exclusively in monetary terms, perhaps because you were wealthy in your country, it will not be easy to feel "successful" in America, using that same definition. Whatever standard of living you achieved in your country, it will be much more difficult to achieve the same thing here. And even if you do, it won't hold the same high status as it did in your country. In America, there are already so many people at that level. It becomes "no big deal."

Some of these "high class" newcomers fail miserably in America. They spend all their money and get heavily into debt. They are often too embarrassed to study English in a class with other foreigners and children, so they never learn. Often they feel lonely and turn to alcohol. And, of course, they become too embarrassed to go back home.

So how else can we define success, if not in monetary terms? Author Earl Nightingale defined success as "the progressive realization of a worthy goal." It is something that is <u>continuously pursued</u>, something that challenges us, something that demands work and excellence. What we accomplish and, especially, what we <u>work hard</u> to accomplish can provide lasting satisfaction, which is what <u>true success</u> is all about.

A college girl who strives to learn and prepare for a career she loves is a success. A boy who works hard on a volunteer project that helps many people is a success. A newcomer who prepares intensely to acclimate to America and build a quality life is a success. These are all worthy goals and marks of true success.

Success is the journey, not the destination. It is the steps and process along the way, not the arrival. And if the journey leads to money, recognition, respect, or fame, the biggest satisfaction will still come from the journey. No matter what you achieved in your country, you are starting fresh in this one. You will need to adopt new thoughts and actions. If you don't shut your mind to new definitions, new approaches, and new reactions, you improve your chances of success.

Study after study shows that what people know they should do is often not reflected in what they actually do. (M. Scott Peck, 1978.) A person may know, for example, that exercising is good for health but that does not mean he will change his daily routine to do it. Another person may know that saving money for retirement is important, but somehow will never get around to doing it. To achieve success in your endeavors or in life in general, you will need to translate what you learn into how you live. You will need to develop the habits and attitudes of success.

Habits and Attitudes of Success

"Excellence can be attained if you: care more than others think is wise, risk more than others think is safe, dream more that others think is practical, and expect more than others think is possible." — unknown.

Where you are in your life today is largely due to your habits and attitudes, which are dictated by your thoughts, of course. Sometimes it is difficult to distinguish between habits and attitudes. Habits are generally those things we do repeatedly. Attitudes are generally the way we do them. What we do and the way we do it are equally important.

The best habits and attitudes to have are the ones that help you effectively maneuver and feel satisfaction throughout your life's journey. There is nothing magical about them. Many are common sense and are applicable to everyone striving for success. Successful people have developed the habits and attitudes of:

- feeling good about themselves and others
- developing a positive mental picture

- sustaining strong internal motivation
- demonstrating high levels of persistence
- upholding their integrity
- maintaining a sense of humor
- improving their physical health
- nurturing their spiritual health.

Let us examine each of these more closely.

■ Feeling Good

"We have to learn to be our own best friends because we fall too easily into the trap of being our worst enemies." — Roderick Thorp.

What we perceive and how we respond to the things that happen to us cause us to either feel bad or good. Successful people have a habit of looking for the goodness in themselves, other people, and life circumstances. They make feeling good a habit. Below are some steps that could help anyone feel better just by looking at things in a different way.

Accept your shortcomings instead of trying to hide them. It may be possible to change certain things you don't like about yourself, for example, your hair color or your weight. However, there will always be a few that have to be accepted as permanent, for example, your hair loss or your height. It is no use lamenting about the things you cannot change. Accept them and think about your strengths instead.

View things in many colors. Rarely are things in life completely black or white. Events are usually a mixture of good and bad. Freedom in my country has brought good things and bad things. An illness may keep you from work, but also give you more time to be with your family. By not getting the promotion you want, you don't have to work the longer hours that would be expected. Something that seems to be a disappointment now, may be a blessing later. Don't look at setbacks as catastrophes. You will feel better if you find what good is there.

Strengthen your emotional intelligence. Marilyn vos Savant, who is listed in "The Guinness Book of World Records" as having the highest Intelligence Quotient, believes that to become stronger emotionally, a person needs two things: to have more experience and to take life less personally. She suggests that if your employer criticizes your work, don't take it personally. Find out what is needed and fix it. If you get robbed, don't waste time and energy thinking "why me?" (Parade, 1994.) Learn something from the experience and move on.

The sooner we accept the things we cannot change, view events in our life more realistically, the stronger we will grow emotionally and the better we will feel. The quicker we move to feeling good, no matter what happens, the more prepared we are for successful, satisfying decision-making.

■ Positive Mental Picture

"If you think you can or can't, you are always right." — Henry Ford.

Each of us carries a mental self-picture. Take some time to think about yours. Your mental picture will effect your journey to success. The next few paragraphs are based on the research of Maxwell Maltz, the renowned author of *Psycho-cybernetics.*

Your mental picture is painted by your past successes and failures and the way people treated you while you were growing up. Once you create this picture in your mind it becomes "the truth" for you. It rules your behavior and personality. You may not even question whether the picture is valid. You just accept it and live according to what it dictates. It becomes your behavior map.

So if you look at the picture and see a failure, you will always find ways to fail. A girl who thinks she is "bad in mathematics," will continuously get bad grades. Even if she studies more and tries harder, if her thinking about herself does not change, her grades will not change. It is as if someone asks her to find an address in Washington but hands her a map of New York. It is unrealistic to expect her to succeed.

To achieve success we must have the right picture of ourselves so that our behavior maps can lead us in the right direction. As our self-picture improves, our chances for success improve. As we have one success, we are often led to another. Success multiplies. Fortunately, imagined success is as effective as real success. Our imagination can

<u>be the major source of our own improvement</u>. If we imagine our success, we are more likely to actually experience the real thing.

The following experiment illustrates this point. Some years back, an experiment was done on the effects of mental practice on improving skill in playing basketball. In the experiment, one group of students did not practice at all. The second group of students actually practiced throwing the ball into the basket every day for twenty days. The third group just imagined successfully throwing the ball and making the basket. All three groups were scored on the first day and after twenty days. The first group that didn't practice showed no improvement. The second group which actually practiced 20 minutes every day, improved in scoring by 24 percent. The third group, which practiced using imagination only, improved 23 percent.

Psychologists have repeatedly shown that the human nervous system cannot tell the difference between an "actual" experience and a "vividly imagined" one. If you are walking in the woods and see a bear, your brain will tell you to run. If, however, it was a person dressed up as a bear and you still thought it was a real bear, you would run just as fast. Your brain would not know the difference and would react automatically. Your perception is your reality. So if your picture of who you are is wrong, then you are being tricked to react to your environment wrong. That is why you must question the validity of your self-picture.

Just as a negative self-picture can be self-destructive, so can an overly positive one. I have met some immigrants who, either through their culture or upbringing, hold strong feelings of self-importance. Some view themselves as very clever and sophisticated, especially when comparing themselves to Americans. They see Americans as naïve and even a bit stupid. Some have even said to me that "Americans don't know how to live." A mental picture of such superiority and arrogance will be damaging to success.

When you examine your self-picture and decide what improvements need to be made, you can make those improvements through mental practice. With as much detail as possible, for a few minutes each day, image the "new you." Close your eyes. Picture it. If you have been disorganized, see yourself as remembering where you put things, never losing anything, being responsible. If you have been fearful in certain situations, see yourself acting calmly with confidence. If you have been overly negative and critical, see yourself patiently looking for the positive. Become enthusiastic about the "new you." Keep practicing. After some time you will be surprised to find yourself acting differently without even trying.

▪ Internal Motivation

"Even if you're on the right track, you'll get run over if you just sit there." — Will Rogers.

Nothing is more motivating than loving what you do. But every job, every goal, every dream has some repetitive, boring, detailed activity. Because all work that needs to be done, must be done, internal motivation is critical to success. It inspires the energy needed to do the work.

Perhaps you may think that this section is the least valuable to you. Afterall, you came to America! You are obviously motivated! You are obviously determined to succeed! If you can package the same internal energy that you used to desire, commit to, prepare for, and actually complete your mission to come to America and apply this energy to all areas of your life, the rewards will be yours. Unfortunately, this is not the case with many immigrants. For some, the internal motivation seems to wither when the initial expectations about America are shattered.

Keep in mind that, you move in the direction of what you think about most. People who think that they will definitely find a good job, probably will. People who think they could be successful, probably will be. Winning thoughts produce internal motivation. The energy comes naturally to go for the goal.

▪ Persistence

"Many of life's failures are people who did not realize how close they were to success when they gave up." — Thomas Edison.

Right in line with internal motivation is persistence, the thing that recharges motivation. All efforts at success are worthless without persistence. How prone are you to saying, "I tried to do it, but it didn't work." Where would the American Olympic speed skater, Dan Jansen, be if he said that after the first try for a gold medal? He competed in many races in multiple Olympics. He lost each one. Finally, the last race in his final Olympic try earned him a gold medal.

The lives of successful people are scattered with experiences of failure. But they stick with it. On some days, your desire for success will seem diminished. The burning hunger seems to fade. You begin to have doubts. Well, don't quit just yet. Tomorrow you may feel different. Feelings cannot be trusted sometimes because they are so volatile. You have to look beyond the feelings to see what is causing them. Sometimes our fears and other people's criticism cause us to doubt ourselves. Other times, we just may feel tired or lazy. We should always be skeptical when our feelings tell us to quit.

■ Integrity

"Rich men and pretty women never hear the truth."
— a billionaire.

Humor break:
A philosopher is talking to a shoemaker: "Tell me, do you keep to the same advice that you give others?"
Philosopher: "No, do you wear all the shoes that you make?"

The hardest principle to define and uphold is the principle of integrity. Integrity includes speaking the truth from your beliefs and experience, keeping promises, and watching out for others. Integrity is difficult to uphold because it is sometimes risky.

American culture overlooks what's called "little white lies," for example, to spare other people's feelings. If you don't like someone's dress, it is not a big sin to say "it's nice." Of course, lies could often have no boundaries. This may be somewhat influenced by culture, but more often it is an individual choice. If you were raised in a culture that tolerates lies, with no severe damage to reputation, recognize the repercussions will be different in this country.

No matter what your culture accepts as a "small lie" or a "half-truth," you cannot have integrity, by its very definition, if you say one thing but do another. What you say must be true to how you live. If you expect people to be honest with you, then you must be honest with them. If you promised to be faithful to your spouse, you stay faithful. If you said you would be there at nine o'clock, you get there at nine o'clock. People who constantly make promises but rarely fulfill them have little integrity. Success will be difficult for them.

Integrity crosses over to other people. How can you have integrity, if you don't try to stop a friend who plans to do something wrong? Integrity demands that you watch out for others and protect those who are weaker.

The demands of integrity are great, but the rewards are sweet. By upholding the truth, keeping promises, and helping others, you uphold your honor, self-respect, and peace of mind. What better satisfaction could there be?

■ Sense of Humor

Remember the earlier advice from the woman with the highest IQ? Right in line with her advice to take life less personally, it is also a great idea to take yourself less seriously. You make a mistake, so what, laugh a little, and then learn from it.

Taking yourself less seriously does not mean that you should take your work less seriously. Your work, your dreams, your growth are all serious matters. They pave your road to success. You are not so serious because you will not control everything. Things will keep on rolling with or without you. There will be surprises. There will be errors. Humor is your vehicle to stay young, gentle to yourself, and sane through it all.

■ Physical Health

"The chief function of your body is to carry your brain around." — Thomas Edison.

Humor break:
I knew a man who gave up smoking, drinking, sex and rich food. He was healthy right up to the time he killed himself. — Johnny Carson.

Your physical well-being greatly effects your mental well-being. In fact, taking care of your body and controlling its various appetites must come first if you are to develop the mental habits and attitudes necessary for success. You will find it difficult to grow strong emotionally, if you treat your body's physical health poorly. The best guide, when it comes to your health and any health-influencing habits you may have, is always moderation.

New arrivals to the U.S. often exclaim that Americans are "so big." And, sure enough, they themselves put on weight after a few months of American food. There is not a shortage of temptations in America, especially bad ones.

No matter how young you are, the way you take care of yourself will determine how fast you will age and how long you will live. Many young dreams will never be realized due to premature death caused by self-destructive behaviors, such as reckless driving, drug addictions, alcoholism, communicable disease, and especially smoking. In the U.S., the total number of deaths caused by illegal drug use, suicide, homicide, and highway fatalities, is <u>fewer</u> than the number of deaths caused by cigarettes. (David Kessler, 1994.) Fortunately, smoking is becoming more and more unpopular. Have you ever met anyone who is sorry they quit smoking?

You will find many bad influences in America, as there were in your former country. You will need to judge what will keep you alive and healthy.

■ Spiritual Health

Our spiritual health touches all aspects of our lives — the people, the work, the aspirations, the satisfaction. Our relationship with God determines our spiritual health. If this relationship is lacking our spiritual health will be poor.

The practice of a specific religion and whatever name we assign to God, be it Father, Yaweh, Buddha, Jehovah, Allah or any other name, does not replace the practice of our love for him and each other. The fundamental teaching of most major religions in the world is practically the same: treat others as you would have them treat you. What will always matter most is what is in our hearts and how we live.

"I wasn't raised to believe in God," is no excuse for how we continue to think when we become adults. You are where you are in life because of what you believe and what you don't believe. This applies not only to people, but to countries, and nations. If you are not satisfied with where you are in life, change what you believe.

Throughout your life, a little voice inside your head, will send you messages — things that you should or should not do. People call this voice by many different names — gut feeling, spirit, intuition, message from God, conscience. Whatever you call it, your little voice is there to help you do the right thing, to keep you on the right path. It is persistent and urgent. As you go against it, it will first send a warning whisper, then you may be hit with a pebble, then a brick, then a stone wall. When you get the message is totally up to you.

I once accepted a job with a company that was dishonest. My little voice tried to warn me. I felt that I did not belong there. I still stayed. The pebble came when many employees left. I saw that, but still stayed. The brick came when I learned that the company's product was overpriced and, through a clever financing plan, the company was able to hide it. I still stayed. The stone wall hit me when they went bankrupt owing me over $80,000 in commissions. I finally got the message.

Sometimes, your little voice gives you only one warning. Unwed teenagers get whispers all the time to abstain from sex. They know they should, but many don't. They are often hit immediately with the stone wall of unwanted pregnancy. If you persistently ignore the little voice, it will get dimmer and dimmer. It is like a muscle. If it is not used it will atrophy. Your troubles will become greater and greater. Hospitals, jails, and cemeteries probably contain many people who merely ignored their little voice. The best policy is to listen to it. Obey it at the whisper stage.

Remember, poor spiritual health may not keep you from attaining success, but it will keep you from being satisfied with it. In this difficult and mysterious life, your conscience, faith, and love are your best guides to good spiritual health.

In summary, the habits and attitudes of success include feeling good about yourself and others, developing a positive mental picture, sustaining strong internal motivation, persistence, integrity, humor, and improving physical and spiritual well-being.

■ Question

1. How do you define success?

2. Which habits and attitudes of success are the most challenging for you?

3. What steps will you take to continue your personal development?

■ ■ ■

Enemies to Success

 "The world is moving so fast these days that a man who says it can't be done is generally interrupted by someone doing it." — Harry Emerson Fosdick.

None of us can be certain how different events in our lives will turn out. Will the results be bad or good? This uncertainty leaves us with a few enemies. Those enemies are worrying, fear, and depression. We will surely meet them.

■ Worrying

"I am an old man and have known a great many troubles, but most of them have never happened." — Mark Twain.

Often people spend a lot of time in self-absorbed worrying and never question its relevance. They just worry, worry, worry. Most of the worries are about things that will never happen or that have already happened.

In your search for success, you will certainly be distracted by things to worry about. There is no way to escape it. If you are worrying about something you can control, respond with action. Do something about it. If it is something you cannot control, stop worrying. Take steps to protect and prepare yourself instead.

The advice of many successful people is that, if you don't want something bad to happen, think about it as little as possible. Worrying can become a self-fulfilling prophecy. The things we worry about, we often draw to ourselves. The boy who climbs a tree and worries about falling, will probably fall. The woman who worries that her husband will be unfaithful may drive him to become unfaithful. Think about what you <u>want</u> to happen, not what you don't want to happen.

The following is one of my favorite humorous poems:

<u>Why worry?</u>

There are only two things to worry about; either you are well or you are sick.
If you are well, there is nothing to worry about.
If you are sick, there are two things to worry about; either you will get well or you will die.
If you get well, there is nothing to worry about.
If you die, there are only two things to worry about; either you will go to Heaven or you will go to Hell.
If you go to Heaven, there is nothing to worry about.
If you go to Hell, you will be so busy shaking hands with friends, you will not have time to worry.

– unknown

■ Fear

"Life is a compromise of what your ego wants to do, what experience tells you to do, and what your nerves let you do."— Bruce Crampton.

Humor break:
A traveler asks a local citizen, "My friend, tell me, if I pass through this field, how long will it take before I reach town?"
The man responds, "If my bull sees you, fifteen minutes. If he doesn't, one hour."

Everyone knows what fear feels like. Like worrying, fear is merely our mind imagining that something bad may happen. We anticipate disaster. If the fear is regarding your physical safety, then you should probably listen to it. If your fear is about failing at what you want to do, then you should probably not listen to it.

Most normal people become excited or nervous just before an important situation. Those emotions could be confused with fear or a sign of weakness. But it is actually pure excitement and a sign of strength if you have prepared well. Before taking that important exam, before doing that speech, before meeting that important person, before going on that interview, the funny feeling in your stomach is a sign that you will do a good job, if you are focused on success.

What do you fear? Is it unreasonable? Does it limit what you experience in life and what you can achieve? Get a grip on it first by acknowledging what you fear. Then, as with worrying, channel it to something productive. The more you do to confront what you fear, the less you will fear it.

Courage is doing what we are afraid to do. That is why we regard courage so highly. There can be no courage unless we are scared.

■ Depression

"When one door of happiness closes, another opens; but often we look so long at the closed door that we do not see the one which has been opened for us." — Helen Keller.

In the **Health, Safety and Other Tips** section, we listed the warning signs of depression. It is worth mentioning again just how prevalent depression is among newcomers. During your adjustment period in this country, you may feel lonely, overwhelmed and stressed out. You may get little satisfaction from new relationships, missing your family and friends back home. If not controlled, this could be a big obstacle to your success.

Some cultures view depression as a sign of weakness. It is not. It is a medical illness and is more prevalent than high blood pressure. Most people, at one time in their lives, will experience mild or moderate depression. In severe forms of depression, the brain actually changes. This type of depression is usually treated with medication.

Pay attention to your thoughts and feelings. Constant negative thinking may bring on depression and other physical manifestation as well. You can help control depression. You can work on becoming more assertive and social with other people. Don't wrap up in yourself, blocking out new experiences and relationships. Drink less or no alcohol. Exercise regularly, especially when bad feelings overcome you. There have been numerous studies that show how exercising alleviates depression by actually changing the chemicals in the brain.

A good psychologist or family doctor can be very helpful in dealing with a depression episode. And always keep things in perspective. Is life really that terrible for you? The following true story illustrates an important point.

Dr. Adolfo Lopez, a respected and talented physician from Venezuela, experienced his deepest depths of despair in America. His marriage was falling apart, his beautiful baby daughter died, his financial pressures almost suffocated him. It was the lowest period in his life, until the day he looked up and saw a paraplegic girl being wheeled into the hospital where he worked. While waiting for the elevator, he conversed with the girl. She could "talk" to him by typing into her computer. When he got to his office, he put his head in his hands and thought about his good fortune—to be able to walk, to talk, to be free. He felt his first peace and gratitude in a long time.

Don't let depression flare up and become a habit. Keep things in perspective. Like fear and worrying, depression is a temporary obstacle, <u>if you work to defeat it</u>.

■ Questions

1. Which enemies to success have you defeated in the past?
2. Which ones are you dealing with now?

■   ■   ■

Satisfaction in America

"I thought I have reached a point in life where everything would be smooth. But it is not. It never seems to get easy." — Sylvester Stallone.

Life is difficult. It is difficult not just because you are new to this country. <u>It will always be difficult</u>. Accept this fact. Life is full of problems for everyone. When you think that other people have it easier than you, because they were born here or they have more money or they have less obligations, you probably just don't understand the other difficulties they have.

How a person reacts to and manages life's problems determines that person's ability to be happy. Most successful people believe that the easiest road to happiness is deciding simply to be satisfied with what they have now, to live in the present, to strive for their goals, and to help other people. I have heard it said that happiness is a side effect. Pursuing happiness does not make us happy. Pursuing something that uses our skills, that makes a difference for others, that helps us "lose ourselves" in our work, makes us happy.

Trying to wish or wait for happiness to come to you actually postpones it. For example, you may say: "I would be happier if I spoke English better, if I had more money, if I was back home, when the weekend comes, when I get a job, when I get married." Do you see how wishing or waiting for something else postpones your happiness to some non-specific future date? You are thinking of what you don't have. You are not satisfied what you do have. Instead of torturing yourself, simply make a decision to be a happy and satisfied person now, today. Satisfaction with what you already have achieved will not stop you from achieving more.

Living your life in the present, being in the moment as you are doing things, is an important step toward happiness. It is hard to control your thoughts, but letting them always run wild nourishes unhappiness, because you miss what you are currently doing. For example, if you are eating a delicious dinner and you let your thoughts circle around some argument you had with your boss, how much will you enjoy your meal? Successful people recommend that you notice life around you, so you don't overlook the satisfaction and opportunities it brings.

Everyday pleasures give you short-term satisfaction. Lifetime satisfaction can be achieved only by the pursuit of your lifetime dream. Maybe coming to America was one of your big dreams. You have made it come true. You will need to believe in another dream now. Your satisfaction with your new life depends on it.

Satisfaction is also dependent upon the relationships we have with other people, our spouse, our family, our friends. How we help other people, even strangers, directly effects our own personal joy. As the saying goes, "we cannot hold a torch to light another's path without brightening our own" (Ben Sweetland). However, that does not mean we look to someone else for our own happiness. I have met many newcomers that have a <u>dependency mentality</u>: "what can <u>you</u> do for <u>me</u>, I'm new, I don't know anything, you know more, help me." Think how much more satisfied and how much more appealing you would be if you thought the opposite: "what can <u>I</u> do for <u>you</u>, I'm here to help, to learn, to be involved."

So, it is very possible to be happy, isn't it? Yes, life is hard. And, yes, you can choose to be a happy person anyway. That is, if you avoid the four attachment traps.

■ Attachment Trap #1 – <u>Craving Money</u>

"A poor person who is unhappy is in a better position than a rich person who is unhappy, because the poor person has hope. He thinks money would help." — Jean Kerr.

Obviously, many people come to America for economic reasons. Putting it bluntly, they come here for the money. No matter what their current economic status, many think that money just comes easier in America. Many become consumed by money, crave it, think about it constantly, do anything to get it. The money is not the problem. The craving is the problem. It is the number one attachment trap and a huge cause of unhappiness.

Yes, money is important and we devoted a whole section to it. However, let us put money into perspective. Would you sell your eyes for $1 million dollars, or your child, or your health? Or if someone offered you $100 million dollars, a huge house, a fancy car, and a television with 100 channels to go live alone on an island and never again be with any people, would you do it? Of course not.

But what if you didn't have to trade anything and the money came for free? Would you be happier then? Probably only temporarily. When interviewed, million-dollar lottery winners consistently say that the first year of their winnings (again, the honeymoon period) brings them relief from economic burdens, lots of attention, extra friends, and the thrill of buying what they want. <u>But then the money does not continue to keep them satisfied</u>. And, in fact, often the money damages their dreams and family relationships.

So are you a bad person, if you came here for the money? No. Just remember that what will bring you the most satisfaction are the things we already talked about, not money. People who always think about money usually chase it further and further away, or lose it soon after they get it.

Whether you have a lot of money or very little, you will still make it. You will still be alive. If you have a healthy, realistic attitude toward money, it will be easier to earn it and much easier to save it. You simply won't spend as much, which leads to attachment trap #2.

■ Attachment Trap #2 – <u>Loving Things</u>

"I won't die lonely, I'll have it all prearranged, a grave that's deep and wide enough for me and all my mountains of things..." — song clip, Tracy Chapman.

The second attachment trap is loving material things. Let's look at the typical life of someone who chases after things.

A young man has a job and lives in a small apartment. He saves some money, buys some things, and wants a bigger place to live. He buys a nice, modest home. He continues to work hard. He makes more money. He buys a nice car and even more things. He decides to move again, this time to a big house. He leaves his friends and neighbors and moves to a wealthy neighborhood where there are big houses. Boy, he can fit a lot of things in his new house! He buys more. He makes new friends. Well, he sees that his new friends have more things than he does. He has to catch up. He works even harder, maybe even does things that he does not want to do, walks over other people, neglects his family, maybe even gets sick from work. But he is convinced he has to buy more things.

Then, suddenly, the man is old. He becomes bored with his things. He gives them away or sells them. He moves to a small apartment and reflects on his life. What do you think he will remember in his old age? Will he remember his first car or his first girlfriend? Will he remember how wonderful his big television was or how great it felt when his little son hugged him? What will be his wishes? What will be his regrets?

When we become attached to material things, to collecting possessions, it is as meaningless and frustrating as falling in love with someone who does not love us back. <u>We may love jewelry, big cars and fancy clothes, but they can't love us back.</u> It is wasted energy.

Don't be trapped by materialism in this land of opportunity. Know what your purpose is, focus on your goals, buy mainly the things that you need to reach your goals.

■ Attachment Trap #3 – "<u>This is the way I am</u>"

"If you always do what you have always done, you will always get what you have always got." — unknown.

There is yet another attachment trap: attachment to yourself. It is one thing to know yourself better. It is quite another to believe that's all you will ever be. This is a trouble spot because it will limit what you try to achieve.

Robert Schuller, the famous Christian evangelist, uses a humorous story to illustrate the limits people often place on themselves. In brief, it goes like this. A man observes a fisherman in a boat. He notices the fisherman catch many fish, but keep only the small ones. He keeps throwing back the big ones. Confused, the man yells to the fisherman, "Why do you keep throwing back the big ones?" The fisherman responds, "My frying pan is only 10 inches."

Have you ever believed that you cannot do something because it's not your personality? Well, your personality will trap you if you let it. For example, if a man feels he can never be friends with a certain ethnic group, he would limit who he associates with, where he works, where he lives. Or if a woman is reluctant to learn how to drive, because women just didn't drive in her country, how much would she be limiting herself in America?

You can avoid attachment trap #3 by <u>doing</u> the very thing you would normally not do. If you feel you must always win an argument, let someone else win. If you like to oversleep, get up an hour earlier. If you see yourself as a big spender, invest the money instead. Forcing yourself to go against your nature takes a lot of self-control, but it reaps great satisfaction.

■ **Attachment Trap #4 – "It's supposed to be"**

"Oh, how bitter a thing it is to look into happiness through another man's eyes." — William Shakespeare.

Being attached to the way things are "supposed to be" is a big enemy to happiness. It is the last attachment trap. Yes, some things we are "supposed to <u>do</u>." It is reasonable that once you have children, you are supposed to take care of them. But it is unreasonable to think that you have to do all the housework, because you are a woman and that is the way it's "supposed to <u>be</u>." See the difference?

You can say that a toaster, a computer and a telephone are "supposed to" work. However, "supposed to" should not be used to anticipate events in your life or other people's behavior. "I'm supposed to be married by now, they are supposed to support me, it's supposed to be done like this, etc." How disappointing when those things don't happen! People and events are too variable to predict. And there are so many different ways to do things.

This attachment trap hurts people especially when good things happen. People can't appreciate it. They believe that it's supposed to be like this, that they are entitled to it. If people help them, well that's the way it's supposed to be "because I'm the youngest, or I'm sick, or I'm new to this country, or they owe me." They will not be satisfied with a little, and they will not be satisfied with a lot.

Enough examples. I guess you see a pattern here. Attachments hurt happiness. They literally control it. If you aim to be happy and satisfied with your new life in America, practice letting go of all four attachments. And always keep in mind your good fortune. The following quote captures this the best: "Just think how happy you would be if you lost everything you have right now and then got it back again." Imagine . . . everything you have and everyone you love is gone. There is nothing left. A whole month goes by. Then you get everything back. Wow! I bet you would be happy!

■ **Questions**

1. What would make you satisfied with your new life?
2. Which attachment traps could cause trouble for you?

Your Family

In America, there are many temptations, many opportunities, many influences, many stray paths. Some of your family members will adjust more quickly. Others will struggle. How do you keep the family together in this new world? It is not easy. It helps to keep in mind the words of author Brian Tracy: "No dream achieved, money or fame gained, respect from outsiders bestowed will ever make up for losses in family happiness." The following pioneer's story illustrates where true satisfaction can be found.

Rudy Paul made a daring escape from East Germany when he was a young man. After short stays in Sweden, West Germany, England and Scotland, he crossed the Atlantic to come to America in 1971. While his friends headed for Australia, enticed at that time by the offers of jobs and free airfare, he took another route. His main reason for coming to the U.S. is the same reason for many newcomers — economics. With the help of friends he found a job at a restaurant.

A major corporation, impressed with Rudy's work ethic and skills, sponsored an employment visa. He fell in love and married an American. After gaining additional experience in various fine dining establishments, he found a partner and opened his own successful restaurant. When asked what has provided him the most joy and satisfaction in his life, without any hesitation, Rudy responds "watching his grandchildren grow up." His success originated from believing in his capabilities, working hard and taking calculated risks, but it was <u>solidified by decisions made out of love for his family</u>.

■ The Most Serious Decision in Your Life

"Keep your eyes wide open before marriage, half shut afterwards." — Benjamin Franklin.

Choosing a spouse. It is probably the most serious decision you will make in your whole life. When I worked as a pharmaceutical representative, most of my customers were psychiatrists and family physicians. These people saw many marriage scenarios. Almost in unison, most believe that marriage is a difficult proposition, but its success could be strengthened by one thing: if the two people have similar backgrounds but opposite personalities.

Background similarities include race, religion, traditions, customs, economic status, birthplace, size of family, and values about family, money, and discipline. Personality differences would dictate that a shy person would do well with a bold spouse, a talker with a listener, a career-oriented person with a spouse that is less interested in a career, a high energy person with a more laid-back person.

Some immigrants come here blinded by the possibility of a U.S. passport. They look to marry an American at their first opportunity, oblivious to the potential problems that could arise from sacrificing background similarities. These marriages may last, but only with great effort and many compromises.

■ Your Second Most Serious Decision

"If you bungle raising your children, I don't think whatever else you do well matters very much." — Jacqueline Kennedy Onassis.

I heard a man talk about his four children. He described some of the mistakes that he made while raising them, actually mistakes that many people make. He related a story about a puppy. His story goes something like this: We get a new puppy. It is full of life. It wants to run in the field, explore, bark, and do all the things that puppies do. We put it in a cage so it doesn't mess up our house. We poke at it sometimes, train it to do some tricks, hit it, make it obedient. When the puppy grows up, we let it out of the cage. We bend down to pet it and it bites us. We scream, "How could you do this to me?! I fed you, provided you shelter, raised you, sacrificed my youth, energy and time! And this is your thanks?"

Even though your intention to come to America might have been "to build a better life for your children," nevertheless, <u>you</u> made the final decision to come. To maintain your authority and your children's respect, you will have to compromise on some things. They will probably adjust to their new life more quickly. They will strive to become more independent, more like their friends, more "American." You may try to pull them back in. You may become very protective.

Again, there are no easy answers. Evaluating whether something is <u>physically and morally safe</u> may help you make better decisions than concluding that "children just don't do that in your country." You may be surprised just how valuable your children can be in helping the whole family adapt to a new life.

▪ Questions

1. What steps will you take to increase your family's success and satisfaction?
2. What compromises are you willing to make?

▪ ▪ ▪

Mission Statement

Mission statements are often written to guide companies in their daily existence. They are written to reflect the values of the employees and the goals of the organization. Just as businesses benefit from a mission statement, individuals and families can benefit as well. Writing a simple, purposeful paragraph can help guide major decisions and solidify the family as a whole. Below is a mission statement for our family. Take some time to create one for yours.

"To live our lives as people of integrity, questioning to make sure that our motives and decisions come from our conscience and not from fear. To continue the family tradition of working to make a difference in Lithuania and in the lives of other people. Most of all to love, to learn, and to grow together, not succumbing to stagnation and welcoming change. This we believe makes a great life."

Closing Statement

"Where we come from in America no longer signifies. It's where we go, and what we do when we get there, that tells us who we are."

—Joyce Carol Oates.

The 80/20 rule applies to many things in life. 20 percent of customers usually make up 80 percent of a firm's business. 20 percent of investments make up 80 percent of profits. 20 percent of employees do 80 percent of the work. Probably 20 percent of the people who read this book will follow 80 percent of the steps to success in this great land. They are the pioneers—the seekers of new thoughts, new attitudes, new actions. Be one of the 20 percent.

May you find success and joy in your new life.

Good luck !

Raimonda Mikatavage

APPENDIX

"Should I overstay my visa?"

Answer:

1. In most cases, if you came on a tourist visa (B-2), your visa could be legally extended only up to a total of 12 months. Student visas (F-1) and employment-based visas all have their expiration dates.
2. Seriously think about your desire to remain here after the expiration of your visa. The psychological stress of being an "illegal" will effect almost every aspect of your life.
3. Overstaying your visa can damage your opportunities to come here again.
4. Remember, you may still be in the "honeymoon" stage of your stay. Read this book a few times. Are you capable and willing to accept so many changes? Talk to other people you trust. Really listen to their advice. No, they are not telling you to go home because they don't

want you to succeed. Yes, some of those people might not know how difficult life is in your country. However, you don't know yet how difficult life can be in America.

5. Understand that the longer you stay here, the harder it will be to go back. Your relatives and friends in your country may envy you and that may give you an artificial sense of importance. The longer you stay, the more you will think that you will be viewed as a failure if you go back. The longer you stay, the more enticements you will find that make you want to "stay just a little longer to see what happens."

6. Write all the advantages and disadvantages on a piece of paper. Keep adding to this list every day. Every feeling, every confusion, everything you like and dislike about America, everything you miss about your country. Which list is longer?

7. Test your commitment by making a plan for your independence. The people you came to visit will not keep you forever. Where will you live? What will you do? Is your plan feasible? Can you afford it?

8. As you are doing this, really get a true taste of American life. America is about independence, individualism and accomplishment. If you have always been taken care of in your country, either by your parents or the government, you will struggle in America. <u>Always keep in mind that even many Americans struggle in America.</u> So how do you think <u>your</u> next few years will be like?

9. If you still think you want to stay, consult with a good immigration lawyer. Ask for a recommendation from your country's embassy. Call the American Immigration Lawyers Association for more information on how to find one, ☎1-202-371-9377. What are your chances of changing your visa status?

10. Since most satisfaction with life comes from our relationships with other people, ask yourself this one final question. Which relationships, in America and in your country, will be hurt most by your decision not to go back?

Valuable Information

Call the telephone numbers listed below for free publications and more information. Many of them have bilingual specialists. Also see **Sampling the Internet**.

■ Education

AmeriCorp; Volunteers in Service to America (VISTA); information on how to reduce your student loan by doing volunteer work.
☎1-800-942-2677

Education Resources Information Center; large education-related database.
☎1-800-LET-ERIC (538-3742)

Federal Student Aid Information Center; information on Pell Grants and other programs.
☎1-800-433-3243

National Clearinghouse for Bilingual Education (NCBE), at George Washington University.
☎1-800-321-6223

10 Colleges that offer a top-quality education at a bargain price.
This is according to *Time* and *Princeton Review*, 1997. Costs listed are for tuition and fees for out-of-state students. State residents pay a lot less.

- Grove City College (Pennsylvania) — $ 6,917
- New College of the University of South Florida — $ 8,461
- State University of New York at Binghamton — $ 8,865
- State University of New York College at Geneseo — $ 8,909
- St. Mary's College of Maryland — $ 9,555
- University of North Carolina at Chapel Hill — $10,700
- University of California, Berkeley — $12,350

- University of California, Los Angeles — $12,401
- Rice University (Texas) — $12,600
- University of Virginia — $14,434

■ Work

U.S. Department of Labor general information and job line.
☎ 1-800-366-2753

Labor Certification Division, U.S. Department of Labor; information on labor certification and work permits for foreigners.
☎ 1-202-219-5263

Job Accommodation Network; information and referrals for people with disabilities in the workplace.
☎ 1-800-526-7234

The Small Business Administration's (SBA) help desk.
☎ 1-800-U-ASK-SBA (827-5722)

Equal Employment Opportunity Commission (EEOC).
☎ 1-800-669-3362

Fastest-growing job fields, according to the Kiplinger's Personal Finance Magazine, January 1996.

- Home health aides
- Social service workers
- Household workers
- Computer engineers and scientists
- Systems analysts
- Physical therapy assistants
- Physical therapists
- Paralegals

- Special education teachers
- Medical assistants

■ Money

IRS tax forms and publications.
☎1-800-TAX-FORM (829-3676)

IRS Tax Help Line
☎1-800-829-1040

■ Legal Services

American Immigration Lawyers Association (AILA); information on local chapters with listings of attorneys specializing in immigration law.
☎1-202-371-9377

■ Health and Safety

American Board of Medical Specialists
Verifies board certification of physicians.
☎1-800-776-2378

Office of Minority Health Resource Center
☎1-800-444-6472

National Insurance Helpline
Information on life, health, property and casualty insurance companies.
☎1-800-942-4242

U.S. Consumer Product Safety Commission (CPSC) Hotline
24-hour recording about consumer product safety, hazards, product defects.
☎1-800-638-2772

Cancer Information Service
Information on cancer research, how to quit smoking, and more.
☎1-800-4-CANCER (422-6237)

Office on Smoking and Health
☎1-800-232-1311

National Institute of Dental Research
☎1-301-496-4261

U.S. Department of Health and Human Services
Information on free or low-cost medical facilities.
☎1-800-492-0359

National Maternal and Child Health Clearinghouse; publications and referrals to handle maternal and childcare issues.
☎1-703-356-1964

National Mental Health Association
Referrals to mental health groups.
☎1-800-969-6642

Depression/Awareness, Recognition, and Treatment (D/ART) Program
Information on depression and effective treatments.
☎1-800-421-4211

National Institute for Occupational Safety and Health
☎1-800-356-4674

National AIDS Hotline
☎1-800-342-AIDS (342-2437)

AIDS Clinical Trials Information Service
Information for AIDS patients and those with HIV infection.
☎1-800-874-2572

Runaway Hotline
☎1-800-621-4000

Covenant House Nineline
Crisis line for youth and their families — homelessness, runaway children, drugs.
☎1-800-999-9999

National Resource Center on Homelessness
☎1-800-444-7415

National Child Abuse Hotline
Provides crisis intervention and counseling on child abuse.
☎1-800-422-4453

Auto Safety Hotline
Provides information on safety belts, automobile recalls, warranties, and regulations.
☎1-800-424-9393

National Clearinghouse for Alcohol and Drug Information
☎1-800-729-6686

National Health Information Center
Healthy People 2000 initiative by the U.S. Department of Health and Human Services. P.O. Box 1133, Washington, DC 20013-1133.
☎1-800-336-4797

To get the **annual crime report** for any state, call the state's police department and ask for the phone number of the Uniform Crime Reporting Unit. Call that number and ask for the Annual Uniform Crime Report (some states may call it by a different name, but should understand what you are asking for.)

■ Especially for Seniors

Turning 65 entitles you to many discounts from parks, movies, golf courses, airfares, restaurants. Ask for your discount!

American Association of Retired Persons (AARP)
☎1-800-424-3410 for general information; ☎1-800-456-2277 for prescriptions.

Eldercare Locator; National Association of Area Agencies on Aging.
☎1-800-677-1116

National Council on Aging; information on family caregiving, senior employment, long-term care, and more.
☎1-800-424-9046

National Institute on Aging; publications on various health topics of interest to older people; some are available in Spanish.
☎1-800-222-2225

Medicare Hotline; information on Medicare issues and Medigap insurance.
☎1-800-638-6833

IRS Forms Line; ask for Tax Information for Older Americans – Publication 554.
☎1-800-829-3676

■ Refugee/Immigrant Assistance Organizations

These organizations provide various services for immigrants and refugees, from rescue to resettlement. Most of the ones listed have representation in the major resettlement communities. They often provide publications in various languages and help explain U.S. immigration law. Call to request additional information.

World Relief Corporation
USA Ministries
201 Route 9W North
Congers, NY 10920
☎1-914-268-4135

Immigration and Refugee Services of America
1717 Massachusetts Avenue, NW, Suite 701
Washington, DC 20036
☎1-202-347-3507

Lutheran Immigration and Refugee Service
390 Park Avenue South
New York, NY 10016-8803
☎1-212-532-6350

United States Catholic Conference
Migration and Refugee Services
3211 4th Street, NE
Washington, DC 20017
☎1-202-541-3170

Church World Service
Immigration and Refugee Program
475 Riverside Drive, Room 652
New York, NY 10115-0050
☎1-212-870-3300

The Domestic and Foreign Missionary Society
The Episcopal Migration Ministries
815 Second Avenue
New York, NY 10017
☎1-212-867-8400

Hebrew Immigrant Aid Society
333 Seventh Avenue
New York, NY 10001-5004
☎1-212-967-4100, ☎1-800-442-7714

International Rescue Committee
122 East 42ⁿᵈ Street, 12ᵗʰ Floor
New York, NY 10168-1289
☎1-212-551-3000

■ **Recommended Books**

(check libraries before buying)

■ *Practical Guide to Practically Anything*, by Peter Bernstein and Christopher Ma, Random House, NY. A great source of consumer information on money, travel, education, entertainment, major purchases.

■ *Hello! USA: Everyday Living for International Residents and Visitors*, by Judy Priven, Hello! America, Inc., 5310 Connecticut Ave., N.W., #18, Washington, DC 20015 (☎1-202-966-9385). Information and resources for newcomers. Great guidebook.

■ *Speaking of Survival*, by Daniel B. Freeman, Oxford University Press, Order Department, 2001 Evans Road, Cary, NC 27513 (☎1-800-451-7556). Understanding vital life areas in beginning English.

■ *Speaking up at Work*, by Catherine Robinson, Oxford University Press, Order Department, 2001 Evans Road, Cary, NC 27513 (☎1-800-451-7556). Workplace topics in intermediate English.

■ *Short Cuts: An Interactive English Course*, by James Mentel, Glencoe/McGraw-Hill, P.O. Box 543, Blacklick, OH 43004 (☎1-800-624-7294). Beginning English text, great for practicing listening, speaking, reading, and writing.

■ *Immigration Made Simple*, by Barbara Brooks Kimmel and Alan M. Lubiner, Esq., Next Decade, Inc., 39 Old Farmstead Road, Chester, NJ 07930 (☎1-908-879-6625). Easy to read guide to the U.S. immigration process.

■ *Citizenship Made Simple*, by Barbara Brooks Kimmel and Alan M. Lubiner, Esq., Next Decade, Inc., 39 Old Farmstead Road, Chester, NJ 07930 (☎1-908-879-6625). Easy to read guide to the U.S. citizenship process.

- *Handbook for Citizenship*, by Margaret Seely, Prentice Hall Regents, Order Department, 200 Old Tappan Road, Old Tappan, NJ 07675 (☎1-800-947-7700). Prepares students to pass the U.S. citizenship exam.

- *Have a Nice Day – No Problem! A Dictionary of Cliches*, by Christine Ammer, Dutton, Penguin Group, NY. Defines and explains the customary language and jargon used in everyday America.

- *What to Do When You Can't Afford Healthcare*, by Information USA, P.O. Box E, Kensington, MD 20895 (☎1-800-879-6862) Lists and describes what medical services are available for free to treat specific conditions.

- *Moving Successfully*, by Tom Philbin and Consumer Reports, Consumer Reports Books, P.O. Box 10637, Des Moines, IA 50336 (☎1-515-237-4903) You will probably move a few times in America. This book provides information on preparing for the move, calculating costs, packing, saving money.

- *Investing on Your Own*, by Consumer Reports, P.O. Box 10637, Des Moines, IA 50336. (☎1-515-237-4903) Simplifies investment strategies in 401(k) plans, IRAs, Keoghs, pensions, stocks, bonds, and mutual funds.

- *Examining Your Doctor*, Consumer Reports, P.O. Box 10637, Des Moines, IA 50336. (☎1-515-237-4903) Describes how to become a more assertive and knowledgeable patient.

- *Strong on Defense: Survival Rules to Protect You and Your Family from Crime*, by Sanford Strong, Pocket Books, NY. A practical safety and survival guide.

- *What Color is Your Parachute?* by Richard N. Bolles, Ten Speed Press, Berkeley, CA 94707. The most popular job-hunting guide ever, updated annually. Especially read Chapters 3, 4, 9, 10, 11, 12, 13 and the pink pages in the back. It is available in seven languages, in other countries (check pink pages of the English version for ordering information).

- *Apply Yourself: English for Job Search Success*, by Lisa Johnson, Addison Wesley Longman, 10 Bank Street, Ste. 900, White Plains,

NY 10606 (☎1-800-266-8855). Prepares English students for today's job market.

■ *The Resume Solution; How to Write (and Use) a Resume That Gets Results*, by David Swanson, JIST Works, Inc., 720 North Park Ave., Indianapolis, IN 46202. Tips on writing a resume.

■ *Resume Roundup, Volume 1: "Blue Collar" Resumes*, by Yana Parker, Damn Good Resume Service, P.O. Box 3289, Berkeley, CA 94703. How to write resumes for work in construction, warehouse, manufacturing, hospitality, and other trades.

■ Recommended Publications

■ *Reader's Digest*, published monthly by The Reader's Digest Association, Inc., Pleasantville, NY 10570 (☎1-800-723-1241). Condensed information, stories, humor, important issues. Over 29 million copies sold monthly.

■ *Bottom Line Personal*, published 24 times a year by Boardroom Inc., Subscription Department, Box 58446, Boulder, CO 80322. Condensed information from knowledgeable sources that cover topics of money, family, health, careers, etc.

■ *Easy English NEWS*, published ten times a year, by Eardley Publications, P.O. Box 2596, Fair Lawn, New Jersey 07410 (☎1-201-791-5014). Educational newspaper in simple English containing explanations of current events, American customs, letters from readers, places to visit, crossword puzzles, and popular idioms. Each issue contains a glossary. An excellent resource for teachers and students of English.

■ *Newcomer's Almanac*, published monthly by Newcomer's Almanac Publications, P.O. Box 1153, Brookline, MA 02146 (☎1-617-566-2227). Newsletter about American customs, values, social issues, and language, especially for families who have recently moved to the U.S.

■ Publications recommended by your country's embassy, especially those that uphold your country's heritage, language and culture.

SAMPLING THE INTERNET

Type the Internet address (the bold-type http code) in the section usually marked "Go" or "Location" on the home screen of your web browser (Netscape, Explorer, etc.) and press the Enter key. The web page will come up. Click on underlined blue text to search under different categories. Click on "Back" icon to go back to previous pages. Some addresses change. You may need to search using a search engine (Yahoo, Webcrawler, Excite, etc). To find a string of words together use quotation marks (for example, "fire safety"). Addresses ending in **.edu** are usually for universities, **.com** for companies, **.net** for computer networks, **.org** for nonprofit organizations, and **.gov** for government agencies.

■ **Searching**

http://webcrawler.com
Search engine with reviews of popular Internet sites by category.

http://www.yahoo.com
Popular search engine, by keyword.

http://altavista.digital.com
The most thorough search engine; searches every word on every page.

http://index.opentext.net
Open text index for searching.

http://www.infoseek.com
Another search engine.

http://www.dejanews.com
Various newsgroup names and recent postings.

http://www.liszt.com
A mailing list of news that can be delivered to your E-mail.

http://thelist.internet.com
A complete list of Internet Service Providers.

http://www.bev.net/computer/htmlhelp
Teaching guide to HTML, language used to set up a home page on the Internet.

■ **Health**

http://www.achoo.com
Search engine that is specifically medicine-related.

http://www.Healthatoz.com
Search engine called Health A to Z.

http://www.ama-assn.org
American Medical Association with a database of more than 650,000 U.S. physicians and links to health information.

http://www.medicinenet.com
Interactive groups, medical dictionary, medical news and drug information.

http://www.os.dhhs.gov
The U.S. Department of Health and Human Services providing information on food labeling, nutrition, infectious disease, health information for seniors, etc.

http://www.healthy.net
Health World's page. Provides access to articles on various medical conditions and medical, dental and life insurance.

http://pharminfo.com/pin_hp.html
Type in a drug's name to get a description of side effects and warnings.

http://www.healthgate.com
Information for consumers and medical professionals.

http://www.fda.gov
The Food and Drug Administration's page discussing drug interactions, cosmetics, food, etc.

http://www.hcfa.gov
Reports on Medicaid and Medicare programs.

http://www.nih.gov
The National Institutes of Health listing of medical resources and latest research.

http://www.parentsplace.com
Specifically covers children's issues, health and other topics.

http://KidsHealth.org
Information about children's health issues: immunizations, asthma, ear surgery, smoking, hyperactivity, etc.

http://www.teeth.com
Finding a dentist.

http://www.nichcy.org
National Information Center for Children and Youth with Disabilities; many publications available in Spanish.

http://www.cancercareinc.org
Support groups, news, helpful tips for cancer patients and their families.

■ **Education**

http://www.utexas.edu/world/lecture
World Lecture Hall contains links to pages created by faculty worldwide. Includes assignments, lecture notes, exams, textbooks.

http://www.ed.gov
U.S. Department of Education offering information to teachers, students, and parents.

http://www.usmall.com/college
Over 5000 colleges and universities represented to assist college-bound students.

http://www.weapply.com
College applications on CD-ROM.

http://www.collegenet.com
A database of hundreds of four-year schools.

http://www.salliemae.com
Information on loans and paying for college.

http://www.finaid.org
On-line calculators that could help determine the possible amount of financial aid; information on scholarships and fellowships.

http://www.schoolguides.com
Graduate school and financial aid information.

http://www.ed.gov/prog_info/SFA/StudentGuide
Financial aid information from the U.S. Department of Education.

http://www.kaploan.com
Kaplan, the test-preparation company, provides information on student loans.

http://www.kaleidoscapes.com/wwwboard
A message board for homeschooling parents.

http://www.exploratorium.edu
Lessons, electronic exhibits, news, and tips about nature.

http://www.ala.org/parentspage/greatsites
American Library Association; selected sites appropriate for children.

http://www.thinker.org
Over 60,000 images of museum drawings, prints, engravings and photographs.

■ **Work**

http://www.dol.gov
The U.S. Department of Labor page offering labor-related information.

http://www.ajb.dni.us
America's Job Bank page. Nationwide listing of about 250,000 jobs by career and region, gathered by state employment service offices.

http://www.careerpath.com
Help wanted classified advertisements from various major U.S. city newspapers.

http://www.nationjob.com
Job listings from newspapers and businesses that can search for positions based on a person's background and qualifications and respond with an E-mail.

http://www.interbiznet.com/hunt
Tips on searching for jobs on the Internet, with many links to job sites.

http://www.vjf.com
Virtual Job Fair listing career opportunities.

http://www.jobtrak.com
A guide to employment opportunities and resources.

http://www.careerbuilder.com
Job listings in major metropolitan areas.

http://www.careercity.com
Specializes in providing leads to technical, management, computer and medical jobs.

http://www.coolworks.com/showme
Jobs on cruise ships, ranches, national parks, and other interesting places.

http://www.sbaonline.sba.gov
The Small Business Administration (SBA) page provides information on resources at national and local levels.

http://www.toolkit.cch.com
A nicely-organized site of resources for businesses.

http://www.bbb.org
Better Business Bureau.

http://www.cashquest.com
Search engine for business opportunities.

http://chamber-of-commerce.com
Directory of Chambers of Commerce.

http://www.att.com/Telecommute_America
Details on the benefits and setup of working from home or satellite offices. A new workplace option that is in demand by many employers and employees.

http://gatekeeper.dol.gov/dol/wb
The Women's Bureau programs and publications to promote women in business.

■ Money

http://www.cuna.org
Information from the Credit Union National Association; can help locate a credit union.

http://www.irs.ustreas.gov
The IRS home page. You can select to print out up to 500 federal tax forms with instructions, 90 tax publications, and other tax information materials. ☎1-800-829-1040.

http://www.sec.gov
The Securities and Exchange Commission providing basic investment information.

http://www.bankrate.com/bankrate/publ/webalert.htm
Helps keep track of interest rates and bank yields.

http://www.financenter.com/newcards.htm
Credit card advice and information.

http://www.cnnfn.com/index.html
CNN financial news, stock quotes, investment advice.

http://www.wsrn.com
Wall Street Research Net helps locate links and information on publicly traded companies and mutual funds.

http://www.ceres.com
Advice from Andrew Tobias, recognized author of investment books.

■ **Major Purchases**

http://www.pueblo.gsa.gov
Consumer information on cars, homes, investments, employment, health, travel, etc.

http://consumerworld.org
More than 1200 consumer resources to help obtain a credit card,
take advantage of discount pricing, product information, etc.

http://www.hud.gov
The U.S. Department of Housing and Urban Development providing information on various programs and housing issues.

http://rent.net
Apartment guide.

http://www.gsa.gov/staff/pa/cic/housing.htm
Information on housing and mortgages.

http://www.ibc.wustl.edu/ibc/mort.html
Mortgage calculator. Enter in your variables and get your monthly
mortgage calculation.

http://www.ired.com
Real estate listing sites by state and country. Apartments included.

http://www.iquote.com
InsuranceQuote Services provides quotes on term life insurance
for many companies. Free quote will be sent by mail.

http://www.edmunds.com
New and used car buyer's guide.

http://www.autobytel.com
Auto-By-Tel page listing cars.

http://www.cacars.com
Calling all Cars page, more info on cars.

http://www.autosite.com
Dealer costs and inventory information on cars.

http://www.kbb.com
Kelley Blue Book listing car makes, trade-in values, options.

http://www.gw2k.com/
Gateway 2000, Inc., a marketer of computers. Information on pricing and configurations.

■ **Travel and Entertainment**

http://www.stratpub.com/shoe1.html
Shoestring Travel, a compilation of letters from readers on cool and inexpensive travel accommodations, restaurants, sights to see and other travel tips.

http://www.travelocity.com
Free access to the schedules of over 700 airlines and lowest available fares.

http://www.amtrak.com
Amtrak Train's routes and vacations across the country.

http://www.nps.gov
National Park Service site.

http://www.si.edu
The Smithsonian Institution home page on the latest exhibits in museums, galleries and the National Zoo.

http://www.scvol.com/States
Guide to the 50 states.

http://www.state.va.us
A tour of Virginia – historic places, museums, communities, upcoming events. For many other states, simply replace the "va" abbreviation with another state's abbreviation. For example: Illinois — http://www.state.il.us, Colorado — http://www.state.co.us. Some states have different web addresses, however. You can search by state.

http://www.mapquest.com
Driving directions from any address to another.

http://www.unitedmedia.com/comics/
Various popular comic strips.

http://www.finy.com/
Fashion on the Internet.

http://www.garden.com
Information on plants and gardening tips.

http://www.readersdigest.com
The most widely distributed magazine.

http://www.comedy.com/jod.html
Joke of the day.

http://www.suck.com
A sarcastic tour guide to the best and worst of the Internet.

■ **English to Speakers of Other Languages (ESOL or ESL)**

http://www.eslcafe.com
Information and resources for ESL teachers and students.

http://www.esl.net/mbt
Multilingual books and tapes.

http://www.tesol.edu
ESL information for teachers.

http://www.comenius.com/idiom/index.html
The weekly idiom for English learners.

http://www.teachers.net/sampler/
A simple web page form for teachers.

http://www.aitech.ac.jp/~iteslj
The Internet TESL Journal.

http://www.ncbe.gwu.edu
Information for practitioners in the field of bilingual education and limited English proficiency education.

http://novel.nifl.gov
National Institute for Literacy and education resources.

http://deil.lang.uiuc.edu/exchange
Stories, pen pals, projects for non-native English speakers.

http://www.cal.org
Center for Applied Linguistics; information and resources on language development, literacy, immigrant and refugee concerns.

http://web.fie.com/fedix/aid.html
Minority information service.

■ **Immigration**

http://www.wave.net/upg/immigration/links.html
Links to many pages related to immigration – translation services, visa information, attorney services, public policy.

http://ilw.com/index.htm
Immigration Lawyers on the web.

http://www.lawguru.com
Legal advice on many subjects.

http://www.nolo.com/category/immig.html
Books on immigration.

■ Government

http://www.fedworld.gov
A gateway to most government bulletin board services on the Internet.

http://www.usdoj.gov
Information from the U.S. Department of Justice.

http://www.ssa.gov/SSA_Home.html
Everything on the Social Security Administration.

http://www.ins.usdoj.gov
The U.S. Immigration and Naturalization Service.

http://www.whitehouse.gov
Information on White House tours, news from the President, message center.

http://www.house.gov
The U.S. House of Representatives information on the Bill of Rights, Constitution, court decisions, hearings, federal regulations, legislation, international law, and many other topics.

http://www.senate.gov
Directory of senators, tour of the U.S. Capitol.

http://www.embassy.org
Electronic Embassy links staff and resources of the Washington, DC embassy community.

http://www.loc.gov
Library of Congress.

http://www.usps.gov
U.S. Postal Service.

http://www.usia.gov
U.S. Information Agency.

http://www.census.gov
U.S. Census Bureau.

http://www.cpsc.gov
U.S. Consumer Product Safety Commission.

■ Miscellaneous

http://www.four11.com
Free national telephone directory that lets you find almost anyone's telephone number or E-mail address.

http://www.ics.uci.edu/pub/websoft/wwwstat/country-codes.txt
Internet country codes list.

http://wwfonts.com
Foreign language fonts.

http://rivendel.com/~ric/resources/dictionary.html
Dictionaries and online translations in many languages.

http://user.aol.com/ishchinese/ishmpage.htm
Information superhighway in Chinese.

http://www.uncg.edu/~lixlpurc/german.html
Information and instructions in German.

http://www.latinolink.com
Spanish-related sites and information.

http://www.travlang.com
Fast translation in 33 languages, especially useful for travelers.

http://www.yahoo.com
A favorite search engine. Enter your country's name with key words or phrases. For example, searching <u>Korean language</u> will list jobs, software, TV & radio programs, translation services — all for Koreans. Another example, searching <u>Vietnamese friends</u> will provide links to personal pages, entertainment, news, and miscellaneous companies and services. A great way to meet and network with people from your country.

REFERENCES

Althen, Gary. *American Ways: A Guide for Foreigners in the United States*. Intercultural Press, Inc., Yarmouth, ME, 1988.

Barrett, William P. "The Best Financial Advisers," *Worth*, October, 1996.

Beardstown Ladies' Investment Club. *The Beardstown Ladies' StitchinTime Guide to growing your Nest Egg*. Hyperion, New York, NY, 1996.

Bernstein, Peter and Christopher Ma. *The Practical Guide to Practically Everything*. Random House, New York, NY, 1995.

Bolles, Richard N. *The 1995 What Color is your Parachute?* Ten Speed Press, Berkeley, CA, 1995.

Boardroom Classics. *The Big Black Book*. Boardroom Reports, Inc., New York, NY, 1992.

Bridges, William. "The End of the Job," *Fortune*, September 19, 1994.

Business Driver. "Don't be a Victim," 1996.

Refugee Service Center. *Welcome to the United States: A Guidebook for Refugees*. Center for Applied Linguistics, Washington, DC, 1996.

Chavez, Linda and John J. Miller. "The Immigration Myth," *Reader's Digest*, May, 1996.

Combs, Patrick. *Major in Success: Make College Easier, Beat the System and Get a Very Cool Job*. Ten Speed Press, Berkeley, CA 1994.

Consumer Reports. "How Good is your Bank?" March, 1996.

Cook, John, compiled by. *The Rubicon Dictionary of Positive, Life-affirming & Inspirational Quotations*. Rubicon Press, Inc., Newington, CN, 1994.

Covey, Stephen R. *The Seven Habits of Highly Effective People*. Simon & Schuster, New York, NY, 1989.

Davis, Peter. *If You Came This Way: A Journey Through the Lives of the Underclass*. John Wiley & Sons, Inc., New York, NY, 1995.

Darbininkas, Humor breaks, from various issues, 1994.

Driscoll, David. "The Benefits of Failure," *Sales and Marketing Management.* April, 1989.

Fisher, Roger and William Ury. *Getting to Yes: Negotiating Agreement Without Giving In.* Penguin Group, New York, NY, 1981.

Frank, Milo O. *How to get your Point Across in 30 Seconds — or Less*, Simon and Schuster, New York, NY, 1986.

Kaplan, Martin and Naomi Weiss. *What the IRS Doesn't Want You to Know.* Villard Books, New York, NY, 1995.

Kessler, David. *60 Minutes, CBS.* Interview with the Commissioner of the Food and Drug Administration, December 4, 1994.

King, Larry. *How to Talk to Anyone, Anytime, Anywhere: The Secrets of Good Communication.* Crown Publishers, Inc., New York, NY, 1994.

Knowdell, Richard L. *Career Values Card Sort.* Career Research & Testing, San Jose, CA, 1991.

Landers, Anne. *Baltimore Sun*, article quoting Judge Haas of Walker, Minnesota, 1994.

Lanier, Alison R. *Living in the U.S.A.* Intercultural Press, Inc., Yarmouth, ME, 1996.

Lesko, Matthew. *Lesko's Info-Power III.* Visible Ink Press, Detroit, MI, 1996.

Levine, Stuart R. and Michael A. Crom. *The Leader in You: How to Win Friends, Influence People, and Succeed in a Changing World.* Simon & Schuster, New York, NY, 1993.

Maltz, Maxwell. *Psycho-cybernetics.* Pocket Books, New York, NY, 1960.

McCormack, Mark H. *What They Don't Teach You at Harvard Business School.* Bantam Books, New York, NY, 1984.

McWilliams, Peter and John-Roger. *Do It!* Prelude Press, Inc., Los Angeles, CA, 1991.

Mirabella, Lorraine. "Buyers from Abroad," *Baltimore Sun*, December 3, 1995.

Nelsen, Jane. *Understanding: Eliminating Stress and Finding Serenity in Life and Relationships.* Prima Publishing and Communications, Rocklin, CA, 1988.

Parade Magazine. "Prayer in Schools: Our Readers Respond," January 1, 1995.

Parade Magazine, Michael Ryan. "An Angry Child Can Change," April 14, 1996.

Peck, M. Scott. *The Road Less Traveled: A New Psychology of Love, Traditional Values and Spiritual Growth.* Simon and Schuster, New York, NY, 1978.

Pritchett, Price. *The Employee Handbook of New Work Habits for a Radically Changing World.* Pritchett & Associates, Inc., Dallas, TX, 1994.

Rehm, Diane. WAMU National Public Radio. Interview with Deborah Tannen, a linguistics specialist and author of "You Just Don't Understand." Interview with J. Cooper, author of "In Search of Satisfaction".

Reich, Robert B. *The Work of Nations.* Vintage Books, New York, NY, 1992.

Rinke, Wolfe J. *Make it a Winning Life: Success Strategies for Life, Love and Business.* Achievement Publishers, Rockville, MD, 1992.

Salins, Peter D. *Assimilation, American Style.* BasicBooks, New York, NY, 1997.

Schapiro, Nicole. *Negotiating for your Life.* Henry Colt and Co., New York, NY, 1993.

Sinetar, Marsha. *Do what you Love, the Money will Follow.* Dell Publishing, New York, NY, 1987.

Spiers, Joseph. "Where to Find Money for College," *Reader's Digest,* February, 1996.

Stein, Benjamin J. "Mistakes Winners Don't Make," *Reader's Digest,* November, 1994.

Stewart, Edward C. and Milton J. Benett. *American Cultural Patterns: A Cross-cultural Perspective.* Intercultural Press, Yarmouth, ME, 1991.

Timberg, Craig. "New U.S. Citizen Trumpets Virtues of his Country," *Baltimore Sun,* May 18, 1996.

Tracy, Brian. *The Psychology of Achievement.* Tape series. Nightingale Conant Corporation, Niles, Illinois, 1987.

Ungar, Sanford J. *Fresh Blood: The New American Immigrants.* Simon & Schuster, New York, NY, 1995.

U.S. Commission on Immigration Reform. *Becoming an American: Immigration and Immigrant Policy.* A Report to Congress, September, 1997.

U.S. Department of Health and Human Services, "Depression is a Treatable Illness," Rockville, MD, 1993.

Vickers, Marcia. "When a Thief Stole My Name," *Reader's Digest,* May, 1996.

Vos Savant, Marilyn. *Parade Magazine.* December 4, 1994.

Wilson Learning System. *Social Style Summary.* Wilson Learning Corporation, Eden Prairie, MN, 1975.

INDEX

About the Author

Raimonda Mikatavage was born in Kaunas, Lithuania in 1962. Her family emigrated to the United States in 1972. She is a naturalized U.S. citizen, who proudly maintains her Lithuanian heritage.

Raimonda graduated with honors from the University of Maryland with a Bachelor of Science degree in Marketing. Her postgraduate studies were in international business. Her career has been in medical sales and sales training. She is the author of two books. Her work with immigrant assistance organizations has been recognized with a Governor's citation from the state of Maryland and she is a nominee to serve on the Governor's Advisory Council for New Americans. Raimonda hosts a television show called "Dreams in Action" for Prestige Vision Channel 3 in Westminster, Maryland. The show explores how individuals achieve their special dreams and lifetime goals.

This book is the result of many years of research in the area of personal and professional development. It is based on the experiences of numerous immigrants and the author's personal accounts of adapting to life in the United States.

Raimonda lives in Hampstead, Maryland with her husband and daughter.

Workshop

Raimonda Mikatavage offers a personalized workshop for your organization. The workshop includes many tips on how native-born and foreign-born employees can work together better, through improved understanding of each other. Raimonda draws on eight years of medical sales experience to achieve a motivating message to cross cultures for better sales results. Add her interesting workshop to your diversity training schedule. Call (410) 374-3117 for details.

ORDER FORM

Please mark the book(s) and quantities ordered

	<u>Price</u> x <u>Quantity</u>		
Immigrants & Refugees: *Create Your New Life in America* (inquire about translated versions)	$14.95	_____ =	_____
Your Journey to Success: *A Guide for Young Lithuanians*	$12.95	_____ =	_____
Tavo Kelias i Sekme (in Lithuanian) (Special order - limited quantity)	$12.95	_____ =	_____

Subtotal $ _____

plus shipping 1 book +$ 3.00 within USA $ _____
($6.00 outside USA)
plus shipping additional books .50/ea + $ _____

TOTAL $ _____

Name and address of person to receive the book(s):

_____

_____

_____

telephone number: _____

Please enclose a check or money order payable in U.S. dollars, adding shipping charges as indicated. (Please add 5% sales tax for Maryland addresses.) Allow 2-4 weeks for delivery.

<u>Send this form and check payable to:</u>

Melodija Books
P.O. Box 689
Hampstead, MD 21074 USA
Tel: (410) 374-3117
Fax: (410) 374-3569

Thank you for your order!